LIQUID REFLECTIONS

Liliane Lijn

PENGUIN BOOKS

PENGUIN BOOKS

UK | USA | Canada | Ireland | Australia
India | New Zealand | South Africa

Penguin Books is part of the Penguin Random House group of companies
whose addresses can be found at global.penguinrandomhouse.com

Penguin Random House UK,
One Embassy Gardens, 8 Viaduct Gardens, London sw11 7bw

penguin.co.uk

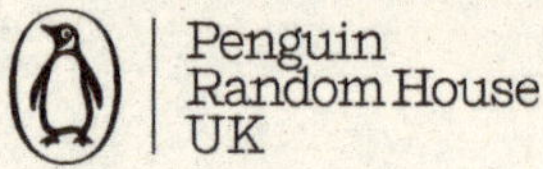

First published by Hamish Hamilton 2025
First published in Penguin Books 2026
001

Copyright © Liliane Lijn, 2025

The moral right of the author has been asserted

Penguin Random House values and supports copyright.
Copyright fuels creativity, encourages diverse voices, promotes freedom
of expression and supports a vibrant culture. Thank you for purchasing
an authorized edition of this book and for respecting intellectual property
laws by not reproducing, scanning or distributing any part of it by any
means without permission. You are supporting authors and enabling
Penguin Random House to continue to publish books for everyone.
No part of this book may be used or reproduced in any manner for the
purpose of training artificial intelligence technologies or systems. In accordance
with Article 4(3) of the DSM Directive 2019/790, Penguin Random House
expressly reserves this work from the text and data mining exception

Typeset by Six Red Marbles UK, Thetford, Norfolk
Printed and bound in Great Britain by Clays Ltd, Elcograf S.p.A.

The authorized representative in the EEA is Penguin Random House Ireland,
Morrison Chambers, 32 Nassau Street, Dublin D02 YH68

A CIP catalogue record for this book is available from the British Library

ISBN: 978–1–405–96747–1

Penguin Random House is committed to a sustainable future
for our business, our readers and our planet. This book is made from
Forest Stewardship Council® certified paper.

I dedicate this book to my daughter, Sheba,
my granddaughters, Nina, Leah, Joy,
Katerina and Kimona, and all young
women who dream of creative fulfilment
and recognition.

Becoming

I am alive because in 1923 my grandfather bought a Cuban passport. Although he was born in the border area that wavered between being Poland or Russia, Joseph Segall lived in Berlin, where he was a shipping agent for the Hamburg America Line. His son Harry met my mother by chance on a Sopot beach, having just returned to Danzig, because the bar he had started with a cousin in São Paulo had failed. Marrying my father, my mother also received a Cuban passport and urged my father to leave Europe and get American papers. Despite being Jews, they managed to travel back and forth as Cubans. Back and forth, because they couldn't decide where to make their permanent home and my father became involved in helping friends and relatives to leave Nazi Germany. Restlessness, homelessness, not quite belonging anywhere. The importance of chance, what my parents called luck. These feelings were passed from them to me and, even before my birth, formed my identity.

I was born in New York in 1939, just three months after my family had finally decided to leave the menace of Hitler in Europe and permanently settle in the United States. My mother told me that for a few months I had a Cuban nanny and that, because of her, my first words were Spanish. I grew up hearing six languages. My father and mother spoke German, especially when they quarrelled. My mother and her mother spoke Polish with each other. My father spoke Yiddish to his father, who also lived with us, and Russian to my grandmother. My uncles and aunts spoke French, and everyone tried to speak English to my brother and me. From the beginning, language was important to me.

My grandmother had a beautiful voice and would sing the pop songs of her time, the sad songs of the Russian idol Alexander Vertinsky. My father also sang, making up his own lyrics and poems, and my brother and I looked forward to the stories he would tell us when he returned in the evening. He had an extraordinarily expressive face. He was large and powerful and full of surprises. You could never take him for granted. Uncles and aunts, from both my mother's and father's side, were painters or musicians, writers or simply interesting people, whose lives were the topics of much talk in our family.

And then there were also shadows. As a small child, I remember people who came to our house and my grandmother would usher me away, in case I said something about the way they looked. Relatives or friends of friends who had been in the camps and somehow escaped or survived. The camps were always spoken of in hushed tones. My mother's favourite cousin, her best friend, in whose family she had lived, sent her a postcard from Auschwitz, writing as if from a holiday camp. I wasn't told this until much later but the emotions that were prevalent from day to day seeped into me and, along with the light of my parents' energy and optimism, I also received their feelings of anxiety and helpless guilt.

When my parents divorced, I was sent to boarding school. I was nine and my father gave me a little diary with a lock and key. I began writing. He also took me shopping for clothes, beautiful dresses that made the pill of leaving home less bitter. But then, only one month after I arrived at Hickory Ridge – a progressive boarding school in the wilds of Vermont to which the surrealist writer and artist André Breton had also sent his daughter, Aube, some years earlier – a seven-year-old child set fire to the main school building and we lost everything. The huge, all-consuming fire that we watched from a safe distance was an awakening. It seemed then that the rest of the school year was spent living in a farmhouse close to the barn with its horses and their smell, close to the feel of the cold snow and ice, the forested hills, where we rode bareback. It was a new kind of freedom and connection to the earth that stayed with me.

Sadly, Hickory Ridge was forced to close and my best friend, Nina, and I were sent to Solebury, a boarding school near New Hope, Pennsylvania. I was nearly eleven and I remained there for the following four years. The reading at Solebury school of Nathaniel Hawthorne's novel *The Scarlet Letter* (1850) awoke in me a painful awareness of the vulnerability of being a woman. I remember the pleasure and excitement of holiday outings to the Museum of Modern Art in New York and the magic of theatre. *Porgy and Bess*, seen as a child, remains unforgettable, as do Sundays at Radio City Hall, with its huge organ and shimmering floor show and the psychological dramas my father took me to.

When I was fourteen and had begun to feel at ease in my surroundings, my father, who had by now remarried, decided to move to Geneva in Switzerland. He took my brother and me with him, but my mother hurried to join us, and I chose to live with her, across the Alps, in the small town of Lugano. There, I attended the only grammar school, a Swiss-Italian state school where no one spoke English. I was unable to communicate, and – having before always been at the top of my class – suddenly felt stupid, although I soon realized there were advantages, too, in not belonging. At the *liceo* I learned to study, as I had never done before, and became familiar with great art, discovering that I lived a few minutes walk from the amazing Thyssen-Bornemisza Collection. After nearly three years spent speaking and studying in Italian, with hardly anyone except my mother with whom to speak English, my grasp of English became somewhat unsure, and my interests turned towards expressing myself in a more direct visual form.*

In the early autumn of 1957 a visit from a childhood friend, Juliet, brought the surprising news that Nina was living in Venice. I hadn't heard from Nina since she had left Solebury in 1951. I'd met Juliet when we both were twelve, during a summer holiday on Fire Island, and we had become best friends. Nina and Juliet had met each other when they were four years old, around a swimming pool in Hollywood. While together in Lugano, Juliet and I sent a postcard to Nina, who responded by inviting me to come to Venice.

Nina, whom I'd first met at Hickory Ridge, now lived with her mother, Manina, a surrealist painter, in a palazzo on the Grand Canal.

She had decided that Venice was claustrophobic and, during the life-changing weekend I spent with her in the autumn of 1957, she persuaded

* These opening paragraphs were first published in an article titled 'My Influences' in *Frieze*, no. 164, 2014.

me that Lugano was too provincial and that to become an artist I had to take my life in my own hands. I decided to leave school as soon as possible, and to meet her in Paris, where we both would study art.

Paris

AUTUMN 1958

I had agreed, finally, after lengthy discussion, that I would enrol in the Sorbonne and the École du Louvre. I had hoped to study art, but my father wanted me to study philosophy or literature, the subjects that he said he would have loved to have been able to study had Hitler and the war not interrupted his education. We compromised on history of art and archaeology.

My father took me to Montparnasse to visit Mané Katz, a family friend and painter of the Jewish Diaspora. As we entered, he looked down at us from a balcony. Large, gloomy paintings of tired men with long white beards hung on the high walls. Making us wait, he made his slow descent and sat next to my father, offering us coffee, which neither of us accepted. The men examined me, and Mané made the usual mixture of patronizing and flattering comments on my growth and appearance. Then my father explained to Mané my desire to become an artist and asked his advice. He began shaking his head: 'For a woman, this is no career. What does she want to be an artist for?'

I met Nina at the Deux Magots café, opposite the church of Saint-Germain-des-Prés, where all the most interesting artists gathered. She appeared older, sitting at a table inside, smoking a Russian cigarette in a long black holder, hair tied back and face carefully made up. She seemed the height of sophistication and very happy to see me. She immediately informed me that we were going to the opening of Max Ernst's exhibition with her sharply witty and beautiful mother, Manina, and her mother's partner, Alain Jouffroy.

It was my first vernissage.* Even in the narrow entrance, paintings covered the wall. The crush was so great that the paintings were quite invisible, and I remarked on this. Manina called out, 'If one cannot seeee the art, the exhibition is definitely a success.' A blur of faces and voices and introductions. Max Ernst's 'invisible' paintings were all priced at around

* The 'varnishing' or opening of an exhibition.

30,000 francs, at the time about $100. I thought they would all be sold at that price, the same as my monthly allowance. But I heard that Max was still living in a small attic studio with his wife, the painter Dorothea Tanning, so perhaps even at those prices, he still wasn't selling his paintings.

Nina and I saw each other nearly every day. She was my guide to both the city and the world of artists and poets. Quite soon after my arrival, Nina introduced me to her close friend Jean-Jacques Lebel. At twenty-three, he was both painter and poet, a revolutionary spirit who, as a child, had sat on André Breton's lap. In a way, he was Nina's guru, although she could be critical of his behaviour. My first impression of him was as a crude and irritating young man, strutting down the boulevard Saint-Michel, not walking alongside but behind us, calling out obscenities. What did she see in him? Thick-lipped, pale blue eyes flickering, a reddened complexion, reddish-blond hair a mess of curls. Stocky, swaggering as he walked with his feet pointed outward. He was not at all attractive. But Jean-Jacques could change his behaviour. He could also be attentive, speaking to me quite seriously, being warm and affectionate with Nina. He would describe with enthusiasm his many projects, the magazine he was working on and his latest paintings, the artists he admired and the poets he knew well. On another occasion, he'd say a few words to us and then look away, as if he had more important things to attend to, more important people to meet. I was disturbed by him.

One evening, as I left the École du Louvre and walked towards the Métro, surrounded by a crowd of students, a French soldier approached me, weaving unsteadily, clutching an armful of flowers. He bowed stiffly. 'Voulez-vous, Mam'selle, me faire le plaisir d'accepter ces fleurs?' He insisted I accept the bouquet and staggered away, humming happily to himself. All the way home people smiled at me, as if they had never seen a girl with a bunch of flowers. I had a strong feeling that this would bring me good luck.

Quite soon after the propitious flower event, I was introduced to the Viennese painter Hundertwasser. I told him I was looking for a place to live, and he said he had an archaeologist friend who wanted to sublet his apartment on rue Chanoinesse, a narrow street flanking Notre-Dame. The archaeologist was leaving for Egypt in a week and would be away for three months. I was eager to have my own place, to begin to take root in this city of infinite distractions, and I immediately agreed to rent it. He gave me a key, generously offering to let me move in even before he left.

I had not been accepted as a regular student at the Sorbonne but asked to sit an exam at the end of the year, which would decide my fate. At first, I attended classes at the Sorbonne and École du Louvre quite regularly. Archaeology interested me and I enjoyed visiting the Musée Guimet and studying in its warm and well-stocked library. The École du Louvre classes were large and impersonal. Often, we sat in the dark, the professor lecturing with slides, the students taking notes. I found that quite difficult, since my French, although conversationally quite fluent, was not good enough to keep making notes while following both lecture and projections. I would leave the classes not having met or spoken to anyone.

In autumn 1958, Paris was a sombre city, its buildings dark with the soot and grime of hundreds of years. Walking in Paris was an olfactory event, from the fragrance of crêpes being fried on a skillet near the Deux Magots, to the stale reek of the pissoir on

the very same corner, past Algerians selling caramel-
ized nuts and the tantalizing waft of chestnuts, the
nostalgic aroma of approaching winter. The Paris I
remember was a mixture of strong odours, sparkling light and long shadows, streets without traffic
lights, horns freely blaring, and a constant undertone
of conversation.

The topography of cities presents itself to me in a
way that changes with time and familiarity. Cities, like
people, are never the same as when first met. My early
days in Paris were largely spent in Saint-Germain-des-
Prés, not to be confused with Saint-Germain-en-Laye
in the suburbs of Paris, where I visited the National
Archaeological Museum and saw the small and dispro-
portionately potent, armless, huge-breasted *Venus
de Lespugue*. It is an understatement to say this tiny
figure disturbed me and made my stomach churn. I
found the fertility symbol (as explained in its caption)
crude and grotesque. But to call it Venus, what did that
imply? Somehow, it spoke to my own, still virgin,
sexuality. Was this what sex would bring? Was this
Woman?

The rue de Rennes, leading to Montparnasse,
seemed to climb upwards towards the old Gare de
Montparnasse that, with its arches and multiple

peaked roof, seemed to me a bubbling glass focal point. Later in that first year, I would walk across the whole of Paris, often late at night, as the grey stone body of the city slept.

Once, sitting in a café on my own, I started speaking with an agreeable young man, possibly a few years older than I was. He told me he was studying agriculture and had plans to go to Africa after graduation. He had a group of like-minded friends who met in the evenings, and he asked if I would like to join them. I agreed and we fixed a date. For a day or two after that meeting, I imagined our possible relationship, dreaming of myself on an African adventure, farming, surrounded by animals. Fantasies took up a great deal of my mental time. If I was not studying or concentrating on something specific, my mind would wander into an intricate world of stories, imagining myself in some idealized role. I looked forward to our next meeting.

The two-room apartment on rue Chanoinesse was up two flights of narrow dark steps, smelling of cabbage and damp. The main room, entered from the hallway, had two floor-to-ceiling windows looking up at a tower of Notre-Dame, a minimal kitchenette built into the wall and a long wooden refectory table with benches on either side. An extra bed sagged along the other wall. To the right, a door led into a very small bedroom. The archaeologist's collection of Hundertwasser's strongly coloured, naive paintings covered the walls of both rooms.

There was no sleep for me on my first night there. My landlord had kindly invited me to dinner cooked by his girlfriend, and we spoke of his impending dig until quite late. They told me to sleep in their bedroom, where I would be more comfortable. Their voices filtered through the thin wall, and I soon realized from the groans and soft laughter and endlessly squeaking bed springs that they were making love.

Nina and I met often, for lunch, for dinner, to go on long walks. One day she invited me to visit her new room on rue Madame. The room was not large, but it had a very high ceiling, and what amazed me was that she could so immediately own the space after barely a week. It was alive with colour, the walls covered with drawings, postcards of paintings and places she particularly loved. She pointed out a large pastel drawing on black paper, saying it was her most recent work, a portrait of me. A large bird seemed to be sucking at a breast. She said the bird was my lover, who nourished himself at my breast. I said it seemed magnificent and, without any hesitation, Nina took it off the wall and gave it to me.

Some days after that, we met on the corner of the Place Saint-Sulpice. She wanted to show me the Delacroix mural of Jacob wrestling with the Angel in the baroque church, where both the Marquis de Sade and Baudelaire had been baptized. Pointing to the offerings of body parts, Nina said Saint-Sulpice was the surrealist church. She then suggested we go to a nearby American soda bar that served malted milks and ice-cream sodas. There, we nostalgically drifted back to our years together in boarding school. Despite our return to childhood, we both felt like women on a great adventure. As night set in, we walked towards the Seine, to her favourite place in Paris. We sat under the bridge and watched the full moon's reflection glitter across the surface of the river like a silver path to the future. Nina spoke of the war in Algeria and how terrible it was. She wanted to go there to join the rebels in their fight for freedom. I thought how similar it was to a fantasy of dangerous adventures that I might have, but she would put her fantasies into practice. Only the summer before, Nina had hitchhiked across the

Negev desert. She shimmered with the intensity of her desire for life.

For Halloween, Manina and Alain were invited to a masked ball in a country chateau owned by the surrealist painter Matta. Nina was going with them and insisted that I come too. We were both thrilled, since so many great artists and poets would be there. The only problem was what to wear. Nina went as a fiery devil, complete with horns and tail. I no longer remember if I even wore a costume. Manina wore a long gown and Venetian mask, Alain his usual cord suit.

We entered a huge ballroom packed with masked, costumed people. The walls were hung high with Matta's paintings, surreal visions of alien worlds in lurid fluorescent colours oddly reminiscent of El Greco. I was awed by their scale, not only their size but also their rendering of the vastness of outer space, although the canvases were also teeming with creatures and claustrophobic. I sensed war zones, embattled luminous creatures, oddly biomorphic insect stick creatures, organic technology of future cataclysms. Nina told me she'd heard Matta was now married to a beautiful young fashion model; that he was a great painter, who had betrayed his best friend, Arshile Gorki, by going off with his wife, for which Breton had excommunicated him from the surrealist group. Now that he had to satisfy his young wife's expensive tastes, he had started to churn out paintings and no longer belonged to himself. I had seen images of Gorki's more lyrical and less violent paintings and could see how Matta might have been influenced by them; or, perhaps as close friends, ideas slid between them. Thus informed, I managed to lose myself among the crowd of 'tout Paris'.

In my small apartment, I had carefully taken the numerous Hundertwasser paintings off the walls and stored them under my bed. I could not live with them. I perceived very quickly that works of art emitted vibrations, some of which soothed and enlightened, while others disturbed or just irritated. I might have enjoyed one of these paintings, but the walls were covered with them, and I felt the layered cityscapes or labyrinthine mazes in primary colours expressed naive emotions and mental clutter. They were childlike, without the spontaneity of a child's drawing, and appeared painfully laboured. Of course, I was grateful to Hundertwasser for finding me a place to live, but I was not the only artist who found him irritating. He hung around on the corner of boulevard Saint-Germain and rue Bonaparte, in front of the Deux Magots, and approached anyone he vaguely knew to show them a brochure of his latest small exhibition. Once he trapped you, he droned on endlessly about his work and its success.

My days were full. In the mornings, I struggled to arrive on time to my classes at the École du Louvre or the Sorbonne. Some days they started at ten and were over by noon and on others they lasted all day or were only in the afternoon. In my free time, I began to prepare myself to make art. In an art supply shop, surrounded by a myriad of different paints, brushes of all sizes and types, inks, oils, pastels, watercolours, pencils, charcoal, chalks, papers (loose and in blocks of many different sizes, weights and qualities), not to mention articulated wooden models and easels small and large, I wanted everything. I was paralysed by indecision, inebriated by the aroma of linseed oil and turpentine, and often left empty-handed. My first acquisitions were a large sketchbook, pencils, charcoal, a pen and inks. I would have liked to have all the coloured inks, but I carefully chose a few. It was so hard to decide exactly which colours I would need.

Nina and I attended a painting course in the high-ceilinged atelier of the painter and filmmaker Robert Lapoujade. We were a small group of about seven, mainly women. He played jazz and African music for us to paint or draw to. We were to feel the rhythms and allow them to flow through our fingers into whatever implement we chose, on to the paper, sound transforming into marks and colours. I was a serious student, finding pleasure in that moment and then almost forgetting it, not sensing at the time just how important that teaching, brief as it was, might be for me, morphing into my later work with words, my attempts to 'see sound' in *Poem Machines* (1962) or the creation of two communicating sculptures transforming my voice into light (in 1983 and 1986). Perhaps those lessons combined with frequent nights listening to live jazz at the Blue Note or the Camé-léon were to become an undercurrent of my visually orientated work. Playing the piano, singing and listening to a wide variety of music had been an important part of my life from early childhood. The year before I left the USA for Europe, my piano teacher had begun to teach me counterpoint, and I enjoyed composing simple melodies. When I no longer played an instrument, I almost always listened to music while drawing or painting or making sculpture. The complex rhythms I heard in a piece of music became a part of whatever I was making. I also listened to stories; readings from novels or non-fiction often accompanied the making of a drawing or a sculpture, weaving part of itself into their fabric.

Living alone presented me with the basic problem of income and expenditure. I was not expected to support myself during this period of study, but I had no idea how to budget the monthly allowance from my father. The 30,000 francs a month had to cover rent, food, tuition, everything. Being responsible for myself was a new experience, and this business of money and how it was spent was a very serious part of it. I had never been given any instruction. Economics was not a subject I was familiar with, nor was it discussed by either of my parents. My father sometimes intimated, when he felt I was taking things for granted, that life, the real world, was not easy, that making a living was a hard struggle; but then, most of the time, he spent that hard-earned substance as easily as water flowed. He was generous, larger than life, prodigal and, in many ways, irresponsible. Going shopping with him was an experience in instant gratification. He had excellent taste and immediately spotted the most beautiful dress or sumptuous sheepskin coat in a store window. Without hesitation, he would enter to buy it, though not before – to the salesperson's surprised disapproval – some discussion over the price, all done in a most charming manner. My mother was more careful most of the time but alternated her thrift with sudden splurges. My grandmother Baba was so abstemious that she seemed to live mostly on our leftovers, despite being quite a corpulent woman. She dressed modestly, hardly buying anything for herself. Money was not a part of our everyday conversations. At dinners or at the lavish Sunday brunches my father so loved to prepare, he would hold forth about politics or his latest favourite writer. We would discuss aspects of philosophy or a recent film, but there was never any talk about practical matters.

Entering the School of Life

The École du Louvre classes were in a high-ceilinged darkened room. The professor (they were always male) showed slides of temples and statues, and the sixty-plus students bent over their desks, writing furiously. I tried to follow and take in the narrative, to imagine the ancient culture he described, but was unable to write as fast as the others in a language not my own. One day I realized that the student sitting next to me was also not writing. There was a small patch of silence, an absence of scratching to my left, and I turned to look. A young man smiled and said, 'Would you like to go for a coffee?'

Joan Gardy Artigas was studying to become a sculptor. He was a Mallorquin and knew Dalí, Picasso, Braque and Miró, all artists his father, the great ceramicist Josep Llorens i Artigas, worked with. He had worked with his father, but he wanted to be a sculptor. He had a real atelier with a high ceiling and a wonderful pot-bellied stove. We talked for hours. Neither of us was fond of the École du Louvre classes. It may have been our lack of fluency in French, but we were tired of the relentless pace of the lectures and the size of the class. We were impatient to make art.

I decided that I had to narrow my focus if I wanted to be an artist. I had to practise. Instead of rushing to classes, I spent all day drawing and experimenting. Influenced by the surrealist method of automatic writing, I applied that to drawing. I thought of it as drawing from my imagination. Instead of drawing outer reality, I drew my inner world. But how does one coax the myriad images swarming inside one's brain to appear on a blank piece of paper? Clean new sheets of paper were untouchable, virgin territory. It was difficult to begin, to spoil their immaculate perfection. It was much easier to approach an already marked sheet of paper or canvas, a newspaper, something already used. That was why I had painted over the canvases that my father's wife, Lourdes, had bought in Geneva from their framer, a Sunday painter. Paintings that I arrogantly thought despicably mediocre had inspired me to let loose my fantasies. I had made use of them before I left for Paris. My deliberate defacing of the paintings she had bought must also have been a way of deleting her presence, making the place my own, like a dog pissing over another dog's traces. Whatever its unconscious purpose, it proved liberating. Had I not taken all the Hundertwasser paintings off the wall and stowed them under the bed, I might have been tempted to overpaint them too, and the world would have lost many a great masterpiece.

I realized I needed to learn to draw before I could paint. Replacing my lessons in Histoire d'Art with visits to the Louvre and the Musée Guimet, I drew from the masters. I liked the *Raft of the Medusa* by Géricault. The diagonal position of the raft and the people on it seemed to launch the painting into the void, giving it an urgent energy. I also went to the Jardin des Plantes and sketched the insects in their cases.

Nina took me to the Surrealist Café, where André Breton stood and kissed our hands in his old-style greeting. We met Egyptian poet Joyce Mansour, whose poems I then read, thrilled to have met a woman poet and yet never managing to speak more than a few words with her. I remember the extraordinary painter Toyen as almost entirely silent. The great surrealist poet Benjamin Péret was there, and a group of younger disciples, painters and writers and, on some days, Jean-Jacques Lebel. I spoke with Péret about *les pipes indiennes*. Breton wrote about them, and I remembered seeing them as a child in Camp Glen Brook, small, ghostly white mushrooms, like flowers. Péret told me that they lived off fungi that were symbiotic with tree roots. Except for that curious conversation, which I recorded in my notebook, I hardly spoke with anyone. Apart from the initial thrill of meeting these almost mythic figures, whose books I had begun to read, Nina and I found the meetings tedious. Both she and Jean-Jacques thought that the creative fire of surrealism was now spent, due very likely to Breton's popish excommunication of so many of its brilliant former members, Dalí, Matta and now even Max Ernst, because he had accepted a prize at the Venice Biennale. Jean-Jacques said they had lost the revolutionary spirit and become mired in the bourgeoisie. Jean-Jacques was a fervent follower of Leon Trotsky, an advocate of La Revolution Continuelle.

One afternoon, Jean-Jacques phoned and invited me to his studio for lunch to, as he put it, see his collection of paintings. I was flattered and excited and completely forgot that I had thought him crude, even revolting.

On the agreed day, which unfortunately coincided with my evening appointment with the agricultural student, I made the trip to rue Caulincourt. Jean-Jacques greeted me genially, explaining that, as he wasn't used to cooking, his mother had sent a picnic lunch over with their chauffeur. Then began a guided tour of his studio. The walls of one room were densely hung with framed works, and Jean-Jacques excitedly told me who the artists were, how and when he had met each one, and even how he had come to have their work on his wall. He spoke English fluently, with a Franco-American accent. French and Jewish, his parents had found refuge from the Nazis in New York. His father, Robert Lebel, was a renowned art expert. So many of his friends and colleagues had fled to New York — Marcel Duchamp, Max Ernst, André Breton — and formed a close community. Jean-Jacques, an only child, would have been underfoot, on laps, entertained and spoiled, a curly-haired, precocious child amusing the sophisticated adults. Having impressed me with his connections, he ushered me into his chaotic studio, littered with canvases on the floor, leaning against walls, on easels, in various stages of preparation. A table held paints and brushes, many still dripping paint, others unwashed, paint hardened, tubes left open. Sheets of paper spread everywhere. Jean-Jacques explained the mess – in the middle of working, no time to clear up – but it was apparent this was his modus operandi, particularly when he spoke about his many interests, both artistic and political. Amidst the disorder, he had carefully laid a table for lunch. He offered me a glass of wine and we sat down and ate the food his mother had prepared.

How did it happen that lunch lasted all day, that revulsion turned into attraction? Was I seduced by poetry, the smell of oil paint, whirling abstractions, the bubbling enthusiasm of his huge ambitions as an artist, poet, revolutionary magazine publisher, by desire, his for everything including me, and my wanting, the hugeness of my undefined longing, focused in that moment on his body, by the thrill and excitement of letting go? It all melted together in my first complete sexual encounter.

Are you a virgin?

Yes.

Don't worry, I won't hurt you.*

He was gentle and loving and, despite my fear of the male sex (that tumour), despite my fear and disgust at the thought of seeing it, I enjoyed sex, fucking – not the word but the act. It felt like liberation. Over and over, he whispered that I looked like a Madonna, his Madonna. That evening, in the velvet darkness, he took me out and we met with his friends. Alain was there and commented knowingly on the dark shadows under my eyes. There was laughter, and I felt delighted by my new status, but simultaneously disturbed by a feeling of being possessed. It was as if, having been embraced, I now belonged to him. This elevated me to a new, more important position, but it also dispossessed me of a part of myself. I felt this days and weeks later when we were together: a focus on my

* This extract and all subsequent extracts are direct quotes taken from my own notebooks.

sexuality so intense that, at times, I was emptied or separated from those parts of myself not giving sexual pleasure. I was all body, lascivious, viscous, animated, absorbent corpus. An opened-out flower exuding pollen, a subjugated domestic animal. Even so, I was proud. I forgot that I had stood up the young agriculture student. I would never go to Africa. I gazed into the mirror to spot the changes that Alain, and then Nina, had noticed. What did I look like to others?

I had an oval face, and my eyes seemed brown until looked at closely, when they turned surprisingly green with a yellow-brown centre. My hair was long and fine, hanging below my shoulders in dark auburn waves, but I wore it demurely braided and pinned up the back of my head. My skin was translucent, the fresh skin of an eighteen-year-old who had never worn foundation or powder. I did wear eye make-up, outrageous colours on my eyelids — bright yellow, lilac or royal blue — outlining my large eyes with dark liner and wearing the same odd colours as lipstick, since that was only found in reds and pinks. I had my mother's nose, small and straight, giving me Garbo's profile, entirely wasted in the art world. My mouth, although nicely shaped, was thin and my chin determined. I thought my lips too thin, not sensual enough. My mother always thought her mouth too large, and her teeth stuck out a bit, making her pose awkwardly for photographs. My front teeth had a large space between them, which a dentist in New Hope, where I had attended boarding school before being brought to Europe, had offered to fix by pulling out a tooth and pushing the rest together with braces. I did not see the point of losing a perfectly good tooth and, at the age of twelve, without consulting my parents, I decided against it. My parents marvelled at my sagacity and thrift, and I remained with the lucky space between my front teeth.

Beneath the turtleneck sweater and beige halter dress, there lurked a surprisingly beautiful body. Perhaps my quiet clothes signalled innocence. My revealed body provoked a moment of awe that never lasted. The excitement, the pleasure, the incredible intimacy of *jouissance* (as only the French know how to describe the coming together of man and woman) disappointingly faded into the ordinariness of the everyday, as a storm of other needs swept the perfect moment into a dusty corner.

We would meet almost every evening. Jean-Jacques came to rue Chanoinesse, or we met Nina at the Deux Magots. One evening, Jean-Jacques introduced us to his good friend the Algerian poet Henri Kréa. Henri had a dark and handsome face, his expression serious and sad. I could see that Nina was attracted to him. The next time the four of us met, Henri brought thoughtfully autographed presents of his published poetry for Nina and me. I remember his poems to his mother, in which he wrote about her as a metaphor of his mother country, both servants to France. His poems were laments, in which pride and humiliation were inextricably tangled.

We had an evening meal together in the cheapest of the numerous cheap bistros, sitting on long benches, arranged in two rows on either side of the room. In one tiny bistro, we paid very little for extremely good meals: a herring starter with potatoes in olive oil; salads with large quantities of fragrant green celery; a celery remoulade, the likes of which I have never again tasted. It was a small, badly lit space, where we sat close together in cubicles. The men spoke excitedly to each other of painting, poetry and politics. They did not address us directly, since we were primarily their audience, but Nina and I broke into their conversations. Nina, now in love with Henri, spoke quite seriously of joining the Algerian revolution. Had Henri left Paris for Algiers, Nina might have gone with him. I listened and joined in their pro-Algerian enthusiasm, but I could not grasp the idea of taking up arms.

We often went to listen to jazz at the Blue Note, where Art Blakey and his Messengers played with other French jazz musicians. I had been listening to jazz since my early teens and much preferred it to the more popular rock and roll. Perhaps because I had played the piano from an early age, I could sense the rippling of the musical notes in my fingers. Jean-Jacques swung his head rhythmically as he listened, never making eye contact, cocooned in a world of his own. I would glance at him and feel that, perhaps, I was not quite taking in the music as I should.

Jean-Jacques and Ferro* had met at the Art Academy in Florence. Ferro was married to the Israeli painter Myriam Bat-Yosef. She was tall, dark and broad-hipped, a no-nonsense woman who,

* Ferro is now known as the painter Erro.

having done her military service, could shoot much better than any of the men. She proved this one freezing night in December. We'd gone to a fair and took turns shooting at a target. Myriam easily hit the bullseye and impressed us by winning a stuffed animal. Ferro could paint anything and, one night, he showed us a couple of paintings a friend had left with him for safe-keeping.

'Guess who painted these?'

'Where d'you get Picassos, you bastard!' Jean-Jacques exclaimed – he knew a Picasso when he saw one, since his father was one of the leading art experts in France.

Once we'd finished Myriam's delicious dinner, Ferro cheerfully announced that the Picassos were his own work. So much for art experts.

Jean-Jacques decided that he wanted to take Nina and me to a popular dance hall, unfrequented by artists or intellectuals. I had not yet started smoking.

On entering, the cigarette smoke burned my eyes. Not that this was an unfamiliar sensation, since people smoked everywhere in Paris, in cafés and restaurants, even in the Métro. I very occasionally smoked one of Nina's Russian gold-tipped cigarettes, more for effect than anything else. And in the small, overcrowded cinemas that lined rue de l'Université, near the Sorbonne, I was choked for the first few minutes by the stale, tobacco-imbued air, then acclimatized as the movie took my attention. But there was something grotesque about the brightly lit dance hall, straight-backed wooden chairs propped against bare, dark walls stained by smoke and time, where women sat, waiting to be asked to dance. Many of the men were Arabs, and there were also couples. I felt very different. I saw rough hands and heard raucous voices. Jean-Jacques made lewd comments about Nina, Myriam and me, laughing scornfully. The abasement of women seemed normal and unnoticed.

Sometimes we visited Al Zion, an American painter friend of Jean-Jacques. He lived near the Porte d'Orléans in a big, dark industrial space and produced large canvases in the style of action painting, emulating his hero Sam Francis by dripping paint down bare canvas.

'Painting should be like balling,' he said as he showed us one painting after another. Balling, screwing, humping, fucking. Was that making love, the most intimate and desired merging of two bodies? I felt the words they considered cool inflicting violence on me. 'I balled her last night' was synonymous with 'I raped the woman'. No matter how gently Jean-Jacques did the act, how lovingly he kissed and slid into me, his words retracted the love he may have felt, and he became a rapist.

Jean-Jacques was certainly not a rapist. Sex with him was both exciting and passionate but he then degraded me with an icy stream of constant criticism. According to him, I spoke too much in a high-pitched voice. He would enjoy telling me that my looks wouldn't last, that I would be all shrivelled up when I grew old. Clearly, he felt that I should only be there to tend to his needs. I began to think that I was merely a menial sex toy. Why did I think I could be an artist? He either didn't bother to look at my early drawings or would discourage me by calling everything I did crap. During the day, I continued drawing, hours of intense concentration, interrupted by our evening meetings that plunged me into the disturbing body from which I wanted desperately to distance myself.

At the end of December, I went to Geneva for my birthday to visit my father, who now lived alone. His large apartment, its terrace looking over both park and lake, was curiously empty. The cheerful yellow carpet in the oversize living room contrasted with a general feeling of depression. My father tried once again to persuade me to abandon my life in Paris and live with him.

'I'll rent a large house,' he mused. 'You could go to the university here and I would invite lots of interesting people.'

He might imagine father and daughter living in harmony together, but I did not. I was soon back in Paris, immersing myself in books found on my walks along the Quais or the boulevard Saint-Michel. It was a delight to walk along the Quais, not yet polluted by cars, wooden stalls backed up against the stone walls lining the Seine. There was always the possibility of finding something special: a rare book like *Les Champs Magnetiques* by André Breton. I made masses of notes on surrealism, agnosticism, the letters of Marx and Engels. I had always read obsessively, particularly European literature and poetry, but I was no longer reading fiction. I wanted to absorb thoughts and information about the real world. I had told my father that I did not need to go to university to learn philosophy or literature. I could read. There were books. And people.

I met artists, poets and revolutionaries like Grandizo Munis, an exiled Spaniard who lived in Mexico. I spent a whole night discussing the pros and cons of revolution with Munis, who, no doubt, would rather have seduced me physically had I not kept up the dialectic. At dawn, we ventured out to find a just-opened bakery for hot croissants. Munis then left, after persuading me to distribute his leaflets in Spain, where I had told him I would soon be going. I was gullible and naive, easily persuaded. Distributing revolutionary leaflets in Spain was foolhardy. In May, sitting in the train on my way to Toledo, the leaflets in my small suitcase, I conversed cheerfully with a good-looking and friendly National Guardsman in full uniform. Flirtatiously, I quizzed him about his political views. It only dawned on me later that he might have asked me to open my suitcase.

At art openings or at the Deux Magots, where we frequently congregated, I met several Italian artists. Enrico Baj stands out as larger than life. Speaking Italian, I told him I would be going to Milan with Jean-Jacques in the early summer of 1959. He wondered if I would take a few small paintings for him. I asked if they were his. He laughed, saying they were by Picabia; he would pack them well and, because I was a beautiful young woman, I would not be bothered at customs, whereas they would surely stop him.

Another Italian painter, Gianni Bertini, visited me. We spoke about surrealism while he looked at my drawings and made helpful comments. When I told him that my favourite painter was Max Ernst, he said I might be interested to try the technique Ernst used to make his frottages. He taught me how to apply a resist by rubbing paper with wax crayons, then applying a wash of colour, either gouache or inks. I made good use of his suggestion in my early works on paper.

In a thin green, spiral notebook I scribbled hasty comments and quotations from what I was reading and reminders of books to read, such as Pascal, *Les Chants de Maldoror* by Lautréamont, Apollinaire's *Le Poète Assassiné*, Gide, Aragon, Rimbaud, the German Romantics. The list was long and interspersed with copious notes and quotations from the Surrealist Manifesto. Fichte's 'absolute idealism connected to a different reality than the ego' foretells my subsequent efforts to shed my own ego.

Two authors and their books are written in the

precise handwriting of my close friend Franco Bel-
trametti, who made a brief visit to Paris. I first met
Franco at the *liceo* in Lugano, where he was a year
ahead of me, doing a *maturitá scientifica*. He stood
out, not only because of his jet-black hair and delicate complexion, but by the way he dressed, usually
in black, always with a bright red scarf. In my last
year there we began to see each other. He was
poetic, quite mysterious, and his Italian father and
Swiss mother were divorced, like mine. On week-
ends he would take me to a bar, just below where I
lived in Castagnola, where a small band played
tangos. Once, we spotted our French teacher dancing, as Franco put it, 'Il tango alla vigliacca!' ('the
tango of betrayal'). Franco studied architecture in
Zurich. In Geneva, where we met before I left for
Paris, he'd told me earnestly that what was important in life was how we acted and appeared to
others. Whereas I thought what was important was
our inner life and how we felt about ourselves, what
we wanted to do, not what others thought we should
do. In Paris, he told me that he'd changed his mind
and now felt that I had been right.

There is such a sense of urgency and excitement in the comments I wrote in my notebooks on

what to read and what I had read, such a mixture of poetry and political manifestos. 'Gasoline' by Gregory Corso, whom I would soon meet. Marx, Engels and Lenin keep company with Jarry's *Ubu Roi* and Jacques Vaché's *Les Jours et Les Nuits: Roman d'un Déserteur*. I was studying even more intensely on my own than when I'd attended the Sorbonne and the École du Louvre.

'By ardent search and shedding of ego's veil, find the one self, the one that is egoless and thus proceed' – so said Shri Ramana Maharshi, and I was determined to follow his guidance.

Jean-Jacques had given me a book about this Buddhist guru and advised me to read it as he had. No matter that I found the pages uncut. He told me I was unconscious, and it was urgent for me to wake up. This was my first encounter with Buddhism. I read about the life of this luminous saint and his teachings, and Nina and I took yoga lessons. Jean-Jacques made fun of us, but I wanted to stretch both body and mind, to learn how to breathe again, to comprehend the value of emptiness. I had already had intimations with a vision of my own transparency as I waited in Geneva airport for my father to arrive from somewhere. This was in the days when one could move quite freely around an airport. The arrival area had a large glass facade facing the landing strip and, in the distance, houses nestled on mountainsides. It was early evening, and the lines of red lights on the landing zone intermingled with the distant lights of houses and the still-faintly glowing horizon. I saw myself reflected in the glass, with airstrip, lights, shadowy mountains and sky contained within me, as if I was transparent and the distant phenomena were a part of me. It was a moment of recognition of my own emptiness and the vastness of a me that could contain an entire world. The concepts I read in this first book on Buddhist thought were already familiar and I felt drawn to Buddhism, as I never had to any other spiritual path.

In February, Nina moved into my apartment in rue Chanoinesse because she had to leave her own room, and Jean-Jacques and I were going to a mountain resort for a week of skiing. At least, I skied. He said he had more important things to do and stayed in the small room we had rented in a chalet. I had very little experience, but I wanted to get away from Jean-Jacques. I instinctively felt that dynamic activity, feeling the sun on my face and the silence of the mountains would give me the energy to survive. It was that bad. Why, then, was I with this sadistic man? My diaries are full of self-blame and analysis.

We quarrelled because I had forgotten to bring something. He said I continually forgot things because I was unconscious. 'Why don't you kill yourself?' he suggested, as if that might be a solution to the pain I felt in being with him.

I sat in the sun, absorbing its purifying rays. I saw the mountains rise out of the valley like breasts, and billowing mounds of snow intimating the sensual forms of my desires. An army of dark pines grew vertically on the mountainside and, when I closed my eyes and squinted, I imagined a dying girl riding a Great Dane. Rocks appeared like sleeping bodies protruding from the snow.

I read Artaud: 'Prendre conscience éxige une force et la mort est une question de force.'* 'Of

* 'Becoming conscious requires energy and death is a question of energy.' This is my own free translation. I am not sure whether this is a correct interpretation of what Artaud meant in this ambiguous phrase.

course, death would be the end of consciousness,' I told Artaud, in the imaginary dialogue I held with some authors as I read their books. 'You are thinking of another "force". I will not become conscious if I die, but I believe that I can become conscious in this lifetime.'

Being with Jean-Jacques was a lesson in being alone. He was cruel and humiliating. He kept reminding me that we are always alone, but he could not live without other people, even for one moment. The next day, we had a disastrous quarrel that ended with Jean-Jacques telling me to fuck off. He no longer saw me. We occupied the same room in silence. I told myself that I had to learn to be alone.

I went up the mountain and on a sun-baked terrace, surrounded by music, couples, noisy happy groups and clunking ski boots, I pulled out my copy of *Les Chants de Maldoror*. Count Lautréamont may be a surrealist treasure, but I found his book difficult to read, like moving through a velvet labyrinth. Perhaps it was the language, although I read and spoke French all the time. Feeling a chill, I suddenly realized it was late afternoon and I was almost alone. I needed to get down the mountain before dark.

I began the descent, finding it more difficult than I had expected, and Jean-Jacques's talk of suicide drifted through my mind as I awkwardly negotiated the steep slopes, slipping on the icy piste. I was alone and it had become very cold. But just as I began to feel anxious that I might not make it, a couple of young men flashed by and, seeing that I was struggling, they stopped and waited for me to snow plough down to where they stood. After telling me off for being alone at that late hour, they helped me, staying with me the whole way down. As I grappled with the difficulties of the descent, I realized that my technique was improving and I felt inner strength return. The mountain had gifted me with courage.

Back in Paris, my small apartment was unrecognizable. Nina had made it hers, scattering her belongings everywhere. It felt chaotic, a jumble of objects, books, papers. I loved Nina, and I tried to understand that she had to bring everything with her, and that this situation was temporary. I didn't say anything, at first, but she could sense my disapproval and tension grew between us.

Also, a friend of hers had joined her. Paolo Lioni

was an Italian-American poet, only a little older than we were. He was tall and thin, gentle and soft-spoken. He had a dark view of contemporary society, and the three of us discussed how to solve the world's problems until morning.

Some days later, an envelope full of money vanished. I was certain I had put it in a particular drawer. I asked myself whether someone had taken it or whether I had misplaced it. This put me further on edge and I made the mistake of telling Jean-Jacques, who immediately accused Paolo, criticized Nina and created an atmosphere of mistrust. I assured Nina that I was happy for her to stay on, but Paolo had to leave. She replied that if he couldn't stay, neither would she. Once Nina moved out, everything changed. We stopped seeing each other, my archaeologist landlord returned from Egypt and I had to look for another place.

I found my next apartment from an advert in the *New York Herald Tribune*. It was in the neighbourhood of Convention, on the sixth floor, furnished in French bourgeois style, and had a strange layout. One entered an entrance hall, to the right of which a double door led to a long and luminous living room. Two double French windows opened on to balconies overlooking the roofs of Paris and the distant Sacré-Cœur. Light poured in from the large sky. I decided this room would be my studio and I carefully transferred the furniture into a large walk-in closet off the entrance hall, keeping only a couch at one end and a table with two chairs, on which to draw, write and eat. The far-end wall was perfect for hanging paper or canvas.

The entrance hall turned a corner and a door on the left entered the kitchen, adequate and uninteresting. The narrow hall continued to a bathroom, also on the left, and a dark bedroom right at the very end. The kitchen and bedroom windows faced an inner courtyard, where an uninterrupted greyness persisted, made interesting by the intermittent appearance of a mysteriously handsome man in the facing rooms. I lived there for the next four months and came to identify the flat's topography with the anatomy of my psyche. I felt relieved that I could close the door to the horror of my dreams, shed my night skin, and travel down the long corridor to the luminous and safe space of my daytime world.

This was in February 1959. There is a double page in my diary, sometime after my return from the disastrous holiday with Jean-Jacques in Val d'Isère, that seems relevant to much of my later work. These may be the first nets and cones I drew that would become recurring motifs of my artistic practice. On the right-hand page, I quote from a question-and-answer dialogue on self-knowledge between Ramana Maharshi and a disciple. Maharshi says that everyone knows their self. His disciple continues to say that he is not aware of that knowledge. Maharshi says, and I have underlined, 'Ce qu'il faut faire, c'est se debarrasser de cette fausse notion du "Moi"' ('What one needs to do is to get rid of that false idea of "Self"'). Opposite, I drew a sphere, three-quarters enclosed in a net; the rest seem more like blocks or separate units. At the bottom of the page are two pointed cones, also contained in a net pattern. An arrow points to the units, or netted areas on the sphere. I wrote:

Each of these a being autonomous, independent, yet each essential to the whole. Slow disintegration of earth square containing life of its own. From behind the people surge.

Poems and disturbing dreams fill the rest of the notebook. There are places that provoke the unconscious, and my new nest – high on the sixth floor, cocooned by the bourgeois odours of warm lunches, the reassuring clunk of the elevator, the empty streets – nurtured alarming dreams.

Dreamtime

SPRING 1959

In May, I spent my days drawing in my luminous studio, often meeting Jean-Jacques for dinner in Saint-Germain and walking back to his Pigalle apartment across a silent, sleeping Paris. When I did not meet him or other friends to eat in cheap bistros, I opened a tin of sardines. I spent very little time in my kitchen. The sink would fill with unwashed plates. I was no longer interested in improving my body or doing yoga. My energy was completely focused on expressing my fantasies on paper. I began to make new friends, meeting them on my own, feeling more confident.

One beautiful spring day, walking across Paris with Ferro, visiting museums and gallery exhibitions, I felt a continuous pain on one side of my lower back. Towards early evening, I told him I felt unwell. At his studio, Myriam gave me some pain-relieving pills and we had dinner, talked till late, drinking glass after glass of wine. Ferro, ebullient as ever, praised some of the artists we had seen and criticized others. I returned home to go to bed, feeling sure the pain would go away, but it slowly intensified until, around three in the morning, I could no longer bear it and, believing that something terrible was happening inside me, I rang Jean-Jacques. He answered sleepily and grumbled I had woken him in the middle of the night. I explained it was urgent, tearfully telling him that I thought I might be dying. He told me not to worry, that it couldn't be that bad, 'just take some painkillers and try to sleep', and hung up. In real agony, I dialled the emergency number. It did not take very long for a doctor to arrive, short and hurried, his breath exhaling his recent pleasures. He mumbled that I had a severe kidney infection, told me to see a doctor in the morning and gave me an injection for immediate pain relief. That knocked me out till morning. On waking, I rang my father in Geneva, who simply said that I should get on the first plane. Always generous, he prepaid a first-class seat. As soon as I was in the comfort of the aeroplane, I felt much better. My father put me to bed in his large room. His doctor agreed with the emergency doctor and put me on a regime of antibiotics and painkillers. When I began to feel more like myself, I sent Ferro a card to tell him where I was. Following that, I received a long, troubled phone call from Jean-Jacques, saying that he had freaked out when he couldn't reach me and had trawled all the Paris hospitals looking for me. He'd thought that perhaps I really had died.

'Oh, baby,' he moaned, 'never do that again.'

Sleeping in my father's bed, I obsessively read Nabokov's best-selling *Lolita*, while he retreated to the much smaller bedroom, usually reserved for me or my brother on our occasional visits.

Back in Paris, I was well enough to visit the Salon de Mai, an important annual group exhibition of contemporary art held in the Musée d'Art Moderne de la Ville de Paris. My diary reminds me that there were about nine paintings that I could appreciate – the rest left me cold.

There were terrible quarrels with Jean-Jacques, who vacillated from intensely dramatic professions of love, when we lay side by side at night, to an indifferent lack of communication once the sun rose. I believed he was a mythomaniac, constructing the most incredible lies and continually revising and changing them.

With people of importance, Breton, Joyce Mansour, Ferro, Sabi, Henri etc. he is expansive, full of anecdotes, information, enthusiasm, interested in all their projects, but with others like me, Myriam, or anyone else he feels is less important, he becomes uninterested and uninteresting.

One afternoon, he told me he was going to meet Méret Oppenheim at the Deux Magots to discuss an article he was writing about her work, and he invited me to come along. He introduced me to the tall, rather masculine-looking artist. We sat on the maroon velvet benches, with our backs to the windows overlooking the square, Jean-Jacques and Méret next to each other, while I sat next to Jean-Jacques. She did not show the slightest interest in me, which no doubt was quite normal. Their discussion was long and animated. I sat and listened, feeling like an invisible presence. Not always but generally when I was introduced to an older woman they smiled and, with a tilt of their heads, turned away to speak with the man. It was quite different when I was introduced to a man.

While I was still living in rue Chanoinesse, Jean-Jacques had introduced me to an artist with the unusual name of Takis. Jean-Jacques prefaced his introduction with a warning about how this undependable Greek took drugs and sat around for hours at the Deux Magots to pick up girls. The day I first met him, Takis sat hunched over a cup of coffee, smoking a strong-smelling Gauloise, wearing a workman's cap and appearing lost in thought until Jean-Jacques called out, 'Hey, you dirty Greek, meet my girlfriend Froufrou.'

Takis nodded and smiled at me, baring his perfectly white teeth, and we sat down opposite him. He announced to Jean-Jacques, in broken but oddly emphatic English, that he would be performing a firework sculpture in the square opposite the Deux Magots and we should come to see it. He asked me what I was doing in Paris. Was I a student? Jean-Jacques jocularly offered some obscene references to my occupation but, seeing that Takis was sincerely interested, I told him I was studying archaeology and learning to be an artist. Takis asked to see my work and, flattered, I invited him to my apartment.

I had the idea to paint on jigsaw puzzles. I thought it would be interesting to buy a large puzzle and paint each piece separately to erase all the usual clues that helped to connect the pieces, and then try to put the puzzle together. Takis was fascinated because he believed that it had something to do with my family history, and he asked me about my family and my childhood. He was the first person I met in Paris who showed a real interest in me. He declared that I was an inventor, that only a child from a refugee family would think of making something so impossible, that I was creating obstacles so I could overcome them. My idea was very original and, if I wished, he could teach me the lost wax technique so that I could develop my idea in three dimensions and cast it in bronze. This promise of learning was the beginning of our friendship and the premise of our relationship.

I began to visit Takis regularly in his claustrophobic two-room apartment on boulevard Montparnasse, where he cooked his wax on a small Bunsen burner and never opened a window. The stench of wax, Gauloises, cabbage, piss and sweat blended into what became my main olfactory memory of Paris. On one of these visits, he appeared more than usually excited and showed me a small metal plate with a nail hovering at the end of a string, floating, trembling as if alive.

'Look, this is my latest invention. Guess how it floats?'

I gazed at this small miracle without seeing the obvious and ventured, 'Did you use mathematics?'

Takis explained that he was using a magnet to attract the nail, but the string it was tied to held it just short, so it appeared to float. He was ecstatic and claimed he had revolutionized sculpture.

Takis had a mysterious intelligence, hidden between his hunched shoulders, in the folds of his threadbare black jacket, that appeared choked by his inability to speak any language correctly or fluently. In company, he spoke little but very directly, his dark, intense eyes communicating powerful emotions. I thought of him as a character from a Dostoevsky novel, Prince Mishkin, the idiot savant. Special, yet at the same time downtrodden, neither respected nor recognized. I found him both attractive and awkward but never for a moment thought of him as a potential lover. Instead, I continued to battle with Jean-Jacques in a love–hate relationship that became more impossible with every meeting.

I had other friends. Elie-Charles Flamand, a mystic poet and alchemist from Lyons, often visited me. I'd met him at the Surrealist Café. He was not very tall, somewhat broad, with a large round head and a high forehead under which darkly intelligent eyes peered out, while a small, neat moustache framed his mouth. He would talk to me of his alchemical studies and read my Tarot, look with interest at my latest drawings, and sometimes invite me to dinner – always at special, typically French restaurants. Hailing from Lyon, he was interested in and knowledgeable about food and wine, and tried to share his passion with me. He also introduced me to Paul-Armand Gette, who worked with typography, using metal and wood-block type in interesting ways. His work was my introduction to typeface as art, and may have been related to the Parisian Lettristes movement,* with which I was familiar. Flamand's interest in matters esoteric was grounded in his scientific studies, and both his influence and that of Nina's mother, Manina, who had introduced

* Lettrism was a French avant-garde movement, established in Paris in the mid-1940s by Romanian immigrant Isidore Isou.

me to the Chinese Book of Changes, the I Ching, were important and enduring.

Jean-Jacques has family problems. His father doesn't want to continue to support him. This is a serious dilemma for him. After so many months of separation, I finally saw Nina. She is living in a loft near the Boulevard St. Antoine. She seems calm and happy to see me. Her paintings are beginning to be wonderful. We sit, she pours tea and tells me that she will have nothing more to do with JJ. He behaves like a spoiled child, she says, he is obsessed with his own gain and poisons other people's lives. He is a hypocrite, the very bourgeois he so hates, swollen with his own importance. The only cure for him, she told me, would be to leave Paris for one or two years and get the poison of ambition out of his blood. Listening to Nina, I know I need to decide. Do I really love this man? If I do, there is darkness ahead, and if I don't, then exit.

Nina told me she was leaving Paris and the art world, fed up with the behaviour of the people we knew. She was going to Los Angeles to study biology, the science of life.

I was often alone in my new apartment, absorbed by the progress I seemed to be making. I had decided to experiment with making my own egg tempera paint. I used fish glue and powdered pigments mixed with raw egg yolks. I loved the chemistry, the mixing. I pinned large canvases on the end wall and began painting with this new medium. I enjoyed its fluid transparency.

But my nights were different. Although day by day I felt more confident, at night I sank into a disturbing mayhem of dreams.

At the end of May I flew to Madrid to meet my mother, and on 1 June we went by train to Toledo to

> see the great El Greco painting, *El Entierro del Conde de Orgaz* (*The Burial of the Count of Orgaz*). The construction is a cross, a split between heaven and earth, below colours [are] rich 'major', above 'minor' colours – neutral grey in between. The lace collars of the 'cavaliers', all identical, accentuate the divide. The whole painted over dark red – transparent white

vestal of priest, light coating of white over base of red, shadows black — red appears through grey cloak of monk, on salient parts of elongated faces, on gold mantle of priest in split, which is pink-dark grey, the Madonna's dress pink — a constant use of white over dark red 'fond' — NB hands = points to think about, to ponder. *Lagrimas de San Pedro*: on the left side — strange enormous white head of bird, claw, wing — incredible.

I spent the whole of the next day in the Prado, whose walls were closely hung with paintings by great artists — Goya, El Greco, Velázquez, Bruegel, Murillo, Zurbarán — but the huge rooms that housed them were silent and sombre. There were few visitors and I wandered through the galleries almost entirely on my own, taking time to look closely at the paintings, although the Prado had little natural light and almost all the works were unlit. In the penumbra, the paintings seemed veiled by a veneer of time. I eventually found Bosch's triptych opposite a shuttered window. I stood in front of it for most of that day, enchanted by his visionary depiction of imaginary worlds, his translucent globes and strange fruit fountains, his gigantic birds and miniature people. My mother had introduced me to his work with a present for my eighteenth birthday of a magnificent book and I had seen *The Boat of Fools*, a much smaller work, in the Louvre.

Bosch, *Jardin des Délices*. When I spotted it from afar, I felt like crying or screaming – bursting from my body. I desired yet dreaded to walk into his world. It is so complicated that one can only look at one small part of it at a time. At the frame on the left-hand side panel, the river seems cut abruptly, but I have the feeling that it continues within the frame, beyond it, beneath the walls of invisibility, secretly, it continues.

I returned the next day and began to make notes and sketches. I asked the attendant if I could open the shutters so that more light would fall on the painting. With additional illumination, the triptych seemed to glow with an inner light, the colours as precise and clear as the wildly imagined forms. This was a work of overflowing fertile invention, an inner world of uninhibited depths, but simultaneously, the profusion of ideas and images, the sheer madness of Bosch's vision, was brought to life by immense discipline, skill and knowledge. I felt sure that the apparent chaos and multiplicity of forms were bound by an underlying geometry. I thought Bosch had arranged all the elements in the triptych into triangulated segments, each segment related to the others, in a magical connective web. It did not surprise me that the surrealists recognized Bosch as their predecessor and named him the first modern artist.

My mother and I then flew to Palma invited by Bartolomeo Buadas to stay in his hotel in Formentor. Tomeo was expecting us — kind, sweet, thoughtful. Although we have very different outlooks on life, something even stronger glows between us. I drew his portrait and gave it to him.

When I was seventeen, I'd stayed for a holiday with my father and his wife, Lourdes, in the Marisol Hotel, one of two hotels owned by the Buadas family, where I first met this charming and sophisticated man. Before I left, he promised to send me the works of Federico García Lorca and I gave him my address in Lugano. He kept his promise, and then surprised me by arriving at our doorstep in the autumn of the same year. He spent two days in Lugano, during which time we fell in love.

I was sitting on a deserted beach the day Nina left for the USA. I felt sad remembering our last meeting but at least we had met again and made up. She had befriended Takis and his friend the Greek cartoonist Minos Argyrakis. She had bought one of Minos's drawings — a fat, bald, unshaven, masked man pointing a gun straight at the viewer. In the barrel was a half-naked girl. I think she had her arms up, as if in surrender.

I was lounging on a hot towel in the soft white sand and was surprised to see Tomeo gingerly stepping across the sand towards me. I knew he did not like the beach, did not like his thin, slight body to be seen undressed, hated the sand and the feeling of the water, always too cold. I thought he could not stay away from me and, to prove it, he agreed to swim with me. I ran into the shallow waves. He followed awkwardly, stretching his body upwards, resisting. I splashed him to break the tension, throwing the dreaded wetness at him. We laughed and swam together but Tomeo soon had enough and returned to dry land, where he spotted some friends. When I returned to my thatched umbrella, I noticed that he was chatting animatedly with two young women who had pulled him down to sit beside them. I couldn't help feeling pangs of jealousy and kept looking over my shoulder to where they were sitting. He seemed to have forgotten me. Perhaps he had not come to the beach because of me. Perhaps I was not all that important to him. To make matters worse, serious period cramps obliged me to retreat to my room, where my mother was having a nap.

I must have taken something for the pain; perhaps my mother gave me a hot-water bottle. I began to feel quite strange as I entered the pain, into a larger, deeper space. I had the sensation of my body growing larger and larger. The pain seemed to be a portal through which I expanded until, instead of being in the room, I seemed to contain the room. This continued; the room dissolved, my awareness enveloped the beach and all the people on it. I felt Tomeo and his friends were all a part of this much, much larger me. An extraordinary feeling of empathy for all of them filled me to the brim. All other emotions melted in the warmth of this compassion. I was left with a lucidity that I had never before experienced. I seemed to be both inside and outside myself.

That evening, I listened to Tomeo playing the piano. I thought of his ambition to become a concert pianist, which was now impossible since he had to manage the hotels because his older brother, who had been groomed by his parents to take over, had eloped with a Jewish-American girl, causing his mother to have a heart attack. As the evening wore on, we were left alone and went for a walk in the gardens. Tomeo kissed me and told me how much he loved me. I knew, although he might have strong feelings for me, we could never be together. His family, his Catholicism, his politics and position were insurmountable obstacles. I told him he was a hypocrite. That he didn't really believe and that he was allowing his life to be directed by others.

I would never meet Tomeo again. I heard that he had married and had children. Sadly, he died on 5 March 1973, in an aeroplane collision over France during an air controllers' strike.

I returned to Paris and Jean-Jacques.

It seemed he missed me terribly, especially when

he imagined I was with Tomeo, and he seemed serious enough to tempt me to marry him. But it did not take long for the first quarrel. He did not include me in a small project, which led me to write:

> This is of no importance, what is, is the feeling I have of not really being with . . . him, of his complete non-acceptance of me as a personality!

When he left for Kraków, where he was installing a show at the Krzysztofory Gallery, I returned to my studio, my paints, myself. To the physicality of paint in the hot summer weather, the invasion of the senses by colour and smell. I painted completely naked, feeling the movement of the colours as I brushed them across a canvas tacked on the end wall. I melted into the paint and became part of the painting.

Takis visited me one morning, stretched out on the couch and spent some time looking at a drawing I had just completed – and later called *The Beginning*. I'd used the technique Bertini had shown me: a resist coat of wax crayons, such as Crayola, on paper, covered with a wash of ink. The resist emerged through the inks as luminous, cloud-like shapes that I then delineated, using a pen continually dipped in India ink. I had swirled the ink wash in a great spiral, starting tight and dense and opening out as it reached the edges of the paper. I then drew what I saw in the mottled areas of yellow resist. The centre was dense and, as the spiral opened out, I drew strange flying or floating creatures detaching themselves into a skyscape of pyramidal shapes. Takis pronounced the drawing visionary, saying he saw in it my crystalline world, luminous and pure. But I saw fire and intense passion, all densely compacted at the centre, with numerous, still-sleeping worlds floating outwards.

I saw a film and went to a jazz club with Venetian gallery owner Paolo Leoni. Like so many of my male visitors, he hoped to get me into bed, and I didn't know how to end the evening, embarrassed to even touch upon the subject. As with Munis, I simply stalled by continuing the conversation. Paolo was not in the least interested in my work and barely glanced at the many drawings, collages and paintings that were pinned to the walls or lay in piles on the table and floor. He, like so many men, shut out women artists, particularly young ones. After he left, I was determined to resume working, but my body had its own ideas.

Jean-Jacques may have been my lover, but I had a string of other male friends with whom I discussed many things: the fate of surrealism; concentration camps in Algeria; fascism in Paris.

Paris was very political. Everyone you asked had an opinion, which they would express at length and with passion. Artists were split into two distinct groups, with any number of splinter groups; very loosely, they were either left wing, anti-government, free Algeria and revolutionary, or right wing, pro-fascist, sold-out capitalist and bourgeois. They avoided and denigrated each other and their respective works of art.

I hadn't given much thought to the plan that Jean-Jacques and I would go to Greece for the summer. Perhaps because I felt uneasy about the prospect of another holiday with my monstrous lover. My father wanted me to take my brother, Dennis.

Ferro told me that the forms in my painting were good but that the background needed changing. He also shared his negative thoughts on my relationship with Jean-Jacques. I valued his friendship and worked hard on my backgrounds, struggling with my desire for Jean-Jacques: perhaps I love to be loved. When I am lonely the object of my desire is not actually JJ. I desire something vague, calm, secure, warm, but is this a man?

July 6th – Tonight, the sky was new and splendid, the clouds all radiant birds and monsters, and I completed a drawing very similar to this! I worked all day, put away first painting. Doing a 2nd of sky, bird clouds and spiritual crystal abode of my being.

I sized another canvas with rabbit-skin glue and used the egg tempera I had taught myself to make. The image was as close as possible to what I had seen in the sky. A huge central figure, moulded in clouds and diffracted light, dominated the sky. Her arms were held akimbo, hands on hips, and through the tri-angle they made, clouds magnified into strange creatures. The sky was turbulent, crowded with cloud beings. The figure, a goddess of some kind, appeared to me as machine-like, insect and bird, a composite of all earthly phenomena. This, then, was the subject of my painting. So powerful, both emotionally and symbolically, that I was overcome by the effort of transferring what I'd seen to canvas with paint.

While waiting for the background to dry so I could continue, I went to a Soutine exhibition:

Marvellous landscapes, crazy, lopsided, tormented, deformed, moving and living, bounding from the canvas.

I also took in Takis's extraordinary magnetic sculptures and other exhibitions, continued to read voraciously, and went often to the cinema. The Chinese painter Chin visited many times, another suitor. He said he could see progress in my work and the subconscious influence of Zen and Tao. He persuaded me that a Zen massage would not only relax me but also give me new energy. I succumbed only once, but soon realized he was heading in directions that superseded the detached rubbings of a masseur.

I was bothered by my painting and depressed by a lack of news from Jean-Jacques. A sexy Indian boy lived opposite me and I had been looking at him for weeks. He would undress in front of the window, pulling off his shirt to reveal a beautifully brown chest, arms, shoulders. That was all I saw apart from his handsome face, but he felt mysterious and exciting. Yet, when he called me one evening, from his open window, I drew back and pretended I hadn't been watching him. Was that inhibition or hidden colour prejudice, fear of the stranger?

My diaries record many extraordinary dreams full of colour and darkness, people I knew and imagined creatures, movement and challenge.

Jean-Jacques finally returned, delayed by a day, and I heard all about his trip in the company of the Jaguers and Henish.

The Jaguers were serious members of the French Communist Party, to whom Jean-Jacques showed great respect. He was involved in *Phase*, a magazine they published. They seemed to think I was a spoiled, bourgeois girl who needed discipline. They told me it was my duty to be more seriously involved in Jean-Jacques's political work. The word 'duty' disgusted me. Their attitude reminded me of the German family in Lugano with whom my mother had left me, who had chastised me for leaving the wobbly egg white: 'You have to eat it. We paid for it.' It was my duty. They used the same constricting words, pressing me into service, inhibiting my freedom of choice. I believed that the only duty I had was to be true to myself. If the Jaguers represented the communist reality, it was not a reality I wanted to share.

The following day I concentrated on my painting, able to feel more a part of it as its three planes of figure, animal clouds and background developed:

There is the essential relation between static and motion, concrete and abstract (floating).

Jean-Jacques said he liked the painting, but our relationship did not feel honest and mutual. I was able to talk it over with Takis, who sees me completely as I am and participates in my vision – told me to develop it completely and not to care for anything else. Pact between us. If it goes badly with JJ, I will turn to Takis for love and friendship.

On the evening of 14 July, Jean-Jacques and I joined the crowd on the Quai near Pont Neuf to see the fireworks. The reason for our quarrel that night has vanished with the noise and sparkling lights.

Swearing loudly, Jean-Jacques left me. After a while, I walked down rue Dauphine and stopped at Le Tabou, a bar where Takis often hung out with Minos, his closest friend. Takis insisted that I have a drink. He would look after me.

July 15th – Incredibly, last night I slept with Takis. I am not yet sure whether I love him. I don't really feel in love with anyone, but I feel happy and lucid.

This afternoon I met Carlos, an Argentine sculptor friend. He showed me his sculpture exhibited at Réalités Nouvelles. It was the best there. Cold abstraction but, nevertheless, very delicate and powerful at the same time. He came and saw my work, was very enthusiastic, great encouragement. His criticism was objective and helpful.'

These friends I made on my own, with no connection to Lebel and his crowd, were lifesaving. They treated me as an equal and respected my work, earnestly requesting my opinion of theirs. I was never good at remembering names, but their faces remain clearly embedded in my memory. Carlos was tall, with a handsome, bearded face and kind brown eyes. Of the many drawings I showed him, he liked one in particular: a landscape entirely composed of an intricate interlocked mass of animals, heads and bodies, fish-like or human, drawn on a diagonal across a large sheet of white card.* Drawing automatically in the surrealist manner, I had pulled it out of my unconscious. Carlos thought it was beautifully drawn and compared its technical skill to the drawings of Salvador Dalí.

I still met up with Jean-Jacques, still quarrelling. He said he didn't care if I left, he admitted he felt no friendship towards me, he attacked my personality. I decided he was sick and that our relationship had to have been more than sexual to have lasted for almost a year.

I kept my sense of freedom and equality by spending time with Munis and his friends, discussing world revolution; by having my Tarot done by Flamand (who told me Jean-Jacques was crazy), which prophesied suffering and despair leading to strength and plenitude; by being presented with an

* *Dreamland* (1959).

eighteenth-century biological print of a female head continuing into a spine that Ferro found on the Quai, knowing it would speak to me, and which seemed to foretell the problems I would have later on in my life.

Change

SUMMER INTO AUTUMN 1959

I didn't see Takis for a while after our 'fraternal' night together in his two-room apartment on the boulevard Montparnasse. That was how he had put it – 'we can share my bed like brother and sister' – but his ideas of how that would take place were not the usual ones.

I liked Takis, but his thin, tall, bent-over body did not attract me. That night spent together had changed the way I felt. Not that I had any amorous feelings for Takis, but his reassurance, his closeness, renewed my courage. He told me he'd be there if I needed him. I told him Jean-Jacques had bought tickets for Greece and we'd be leaving Paris in a few days. Takis was himself leaving for Venice, staying at Montin, a restaurant I had visited with Nina in what seemed like a time before time.

'Come if you want to. I will wait for you there.'

It was time to leave my apartment. I had to pack up all my belongings, all the works on paper and canvas that I had made there or brought with me. I had to clean it and replace the furniture as it had been. My landlady had made the mistake of turning up ahead of time and shrieked in horror. I placated her with some difficulty, assuring her that all would be as it had been. She left, not wholly convinced by my promises. Nevertheless, I was an honest and well-brought-up young woman, determined to reinstate her tidy bourgeois interior.

On 22 July I met Jean-Jacques at the Gare de Lyon to board the overnight train to Milan. I got no sleep in our couchette, with Jean-Jacques and I on one side, two men on the opposite side. Jean-Jacques thought it very funny to suggest that one or other of the occupants might take advantage of me during the night and kept making lewd remarks to that effect. I realized this would never stop and resolved once again to leave him.

The next day my determination lapsed. We visited Arturo Schwarz's bookshop and gallery. Jean-Jacques was working with Arturo on an exhibition of inter-national surrealist artists. I was pleased to meet Arturo, since I knew that he was a polymath scholar, poet and publisher, with a great collection of Dada and surrealist works. He was also Jewish and a philanthropist, who gave most of his large collection to museums.

Munis, with whom I'd enjoyed lively discussions in Paris, and E. L. T. Mesens (the poet, gallerist and close friend of Magritte), arrived at the gallery with a few other surrealists, and a group photo was taken. Jean-Jacques said it must have been the last photograph taken of the surrealist group. Arturo is smiling happily. The only other woman in the photograph, standing in the opposite corner to me, hands in pockets, is Anna Seghers, companion of the poet and writer Jean-Louis Bédouin. I am standing with a bit of my left arm and leg out of frame, leaning on Mesens's shoulder, while Jean-Jacques appears to look up at me.

Later that afternoon, I took the train for Venice, promising Jean-Jacques that I would meet him at the ferry terminal late the same evening for the midnight boat to Greece. On the train, I felt free and excited, happy to be on my own, although my mind was not yet made up about whether I would really leave Jean-Jacques. In Venice, I went straight to Locanda Montin. Although it wasn't a hotel, they did rent out a few rooms, often to artists. The owner's son, Adriano, remembered me from my visit with Nina two years earlier and sent me upstairs. Takis was in the shower. Quite naturally, he invited me in.

I met Jean-Jacques as I had promised at the ferry, where I told him I couldn't come with him, that his behaviour in the train to Milan had been the last straw. He pleaded with me and complained that his mother had even bought my ticket.

Takis was in love with me, and I was in love with being loved. I was a relatively inexperienced nineteen, and he was thirty-four, with a rich and dramatic past. Jean-Jacques had continually berated me for talking too much. Takis said my chatter was a delight, making him feel young and alive.

He took me everywhere in Venice, introducing me to friends and patrons. Peggy Guggenheim was the subject of much gossip in Venice and beyond, because of her wealth and straightforward attitude to men and sex. She walked us around her fabulous collection, and it was clear to me that, had she been a man, there would have been more praise and admiration than outrage and gossip.

Peggy's daughter, Pegeen, made obsessive,

childlike paintings, maybe in a desperate attempt to attract her mother's attention. We visited her in hospital where she was recovering, heavily sedated and bandaged, from having slit her wrists. Her husband, Ralph Romney, hovered in a haze of alcoholic concern. Takis told me that he'd had a short affair with her when she was married to the French painter Jean Hélion.

When I suggested we visit museums, Takis took me instead to Torcello, where we made love in the grass in the darkening dusk. We walked along the Riva degli Schiavoni, and I took him to see the Carpaccio paintings that Nina had shown me and then the huge Tintorettos in the Scuola Grande di San Rocco. Takis was unimpressed; he didn't like the Renaissance and said museums were for students. His lack of interest was disappointing since I was passionate about looking at art from all periods.

We went to see Manina, and Takis bought me a silver necklace made by her friend the brilliant Cuban jeweller Domingo de la Cueva. I asked about Nina. Manina remarked, in her particularly incisive voice, that Nina had been pressured into leaving Paris by her uncle, who held the purse strings of her paternal inheritance. 'He wanted to put distance between us. He said I was a bad influence on my own daughter, that she needed to go to university and get a degree. Now we write long letters to each other nearly every day.' She looked at me with her Egyptian-painted eyes. 'You must also miss my brilliant daughter.'

I had frightening dreams, in which Takis appeared monstrous and ghoul-like, an image of death. I woke in a sweat, to see him upright in bed, watching me and smoking. I began to smoke. As I got to know Takis better, my fantasy faded of him as the holy fool Prince Mishkin, replaced by a more interesting and complex reality. Despite little talent for languages, Takis expressed himself with great charm and clarity, perhaps because he knew what he wanted to say. In our first days in Venice, he told me fascinating stories about his adventures, during and after the war, his family, his mad Athenian friends, and meeting his American patron, Caresse Crosby, through the English painter John Craxton. She had paid for his trip to Paris and given him a monthly stipend.

During the war, he'd hoped to join his dead brother's friends, who were all partisans in the mountains, but was unable to reach them. He dreamed of being heroic, like them, like his older brother, who had starved himself to death rather than watch the German army march into Athens. Takis was arrested as a communist, beaten on the soles of his feet and thrown into a windowless cell, told that no one would know where he was. The fascists interrogated him, they wanted names. He didn't speak. At night, he heard screams of other prisoners. He lost track of time and, finally, he decided that he was not, nor ever would be, a hero. Instead, he allowed himself to become an artist.

We took a train to Naples, where Takis struggled with my two large suitcases, mistrusting the many offers of assistance, and then on to Palermo, which I remember as grey and impoverished, then Agrigento, where we stayed in a run-down hotel, the only one near the beach.

August 8th — I have never yet known so much happiness. We complete each other, we are part of one dream. Our two worlds are one. Takis sees me completely as I am and knows how to help me grow and develop.

I rang my father, who would be worrying about me. My rapturous assertions of great love were greeted with suspicion and my thoughtful call resulted in him sending my mother to stay with us, along with my teenage brother, Dennis. Takis accepted them with amused patience.

Agrigento was idyllic, no tourists and few other visitors. Our hotel and the long, paved walk along the adjacent sandy beach were empty. Almost daily, we visited Greek temples near the sea, surrounded by groves of palms and prickly pears. The locals spoke a dialect that Takis understood and said was close to Greek. After we all had lunch together, Takis and I would retire to our room for a nap while Dennis would sneak around outside trying to peer into our window, his shadow glistening in the heat.

After the luminosity of the Sicilian summer, Paris appeared bleak, a sepia-tinged grey. August was the month when Parisians emptied the city, heading towards their holiday venues. I felt a strange stillness in the summer city, where leaves had already turned yellow and begun to fall. Boulevard Montparnasse was desolate, most stores were shuttered, cafés and restaurants closed. It was as if we were the only people there. I felt strangely excited, looking forward to the adventure that lay ahead.

Takis had brought Raymondos from Athens. He was an uneducated garage mechanic, secretly dreaming of becoming an artist, and Takis promised him a new life if he agreed to work for him. In Athens, he had lived with his mother, to whom he was very attached. He was short, stocky and muscular from years of hard work. His face was lined and narrow; his mouth always seemed puckered in questioning hesitation. His brown hair, rarely washed, was always gelled, and fastidiously combed with a side parting. He was careful to appear clean and respectable and stood erect and proud. He was secretive and his French so minimal that, although we lived together in Takis's two small rooms, I knew only what Takis told me about him and never learned his last name.

The apartment was up four floors, in a nondescript building near Denfert-Rochereau and the excellent restaurant La Closerie des Lilas. The front room was kitchen and studio, with Raymondos's cot. Takis and I occupied the back room. The small, claustrophobic rooms were stuffy and reeked of wax and Gauloises, since both men smoked incessantly.

With September, Paris began to awaken from its summer slumber. We realized then that many of our former friends were no longer talking to us. The word was that Takis had stolen Jean-Jacques's girlfriend. Stolen me, as if I had no will of my own, as if I were an object to be possessed. The thought infuriated me. The rumour was that Jean-Jacques had tried to kill himself with a large dose of pills – obviously not large enough. He wept and complained to all and sundry of my cruelty and his friend's betrayal. Ferro and Myriam, with whom I had been close, would not speak to me. Once, I spotted Jean-Jacques in the Deux Magots, and he pretended not to see me. I felt physically disturbed at the sight of him. Takis and I now hung out mainly in Montparnasse, at the Select and the Coupole.

I soon found a larger apartment in rue Leopold Robert, a small side street very near the Coupole. It looked out on a dank, dark courtyard but had two reasonably large rooms and a separate small kitchen. Takis and I slept in a large double bed in the back room, where I also worked, spreading long sheets of paper over the floor. Raymondos slept on a day bed in the other room, where there was also an old upright piano. At night, he used to draw the blinds and attempt to teach himself to play. When I asked why he drew the blinds, he replied that he didn't want the neighbours to see him.

'But they will hear you anyway.'

'Yes, but if they don't see me, they won't know who is playing.'

Raymondos had begun to carve rough-hewn angels from wood, rubbing them black with shoe polish. He always whistled while he worked, shirt-sleeves carefully rolled up. He kept his best suit for Sunday afternoons, when he sat with one cup of coffee and his Greek paper in a small neighbour-hood café, hoping to meet someone of interest.

The Musée Cernuschi had an exhibition of horizontal Chinese scrolls depicting huge landscapes in which people and their palaces were drawn as a small part of the natural environment. I liked their way of viewing the world and the long, horizontal format, unfolding in continuous stories. Some filled the length of an entire wall. I would never come across these extraordinary scrolls again, since most Chinese scrolls seem to be vertical. I was inspired to draw on a larger scale.

I bought a large roll of good strong paper and

started my series of *Sky Scrolls*. Applying the same resist technique that I had used to create *The Beginning*, the work that Takis had called visionary, I rubbed wax crayons in light colours on to the paper and then covered it with a gouache wash, usually in darker blues blending into reds and purple. Where the wax protected the paper, the gouache didn't sink in, leaving indefinite cloud-like shapes that triggered my imagination. On these long sheets of paper, the luminous resist transformed into landscape and clouds, and in the later drawings, strange floating creatures, which I outlined with a pen dipped in India ink.

I spent whole days immersed in the details of my ink drawings, against a background of Kabuki music on vinyl records that I had bought at Sam Goody's, during my last visit to New York, the summer before coming to Paris. I had quite a large collection of what was then called ethnic music – Japanese, Indian and African. When I liked a particular recording, I would play it over and over, often for the entire day. My whole being would be immersed in the sound, creating a trance-like mood. I often thought that I travelled in my drawings, the movement of my pen taking me to other worlds.

I had learned how to draw using a pen dipped in India ink. At first, it was hard to control. I tried to draw fine parallel lines, placing them closer and closer, avoiding them touching or blurring into each other. This gave me the ability to draw what and as I wished. I didn't want to draw what I saw around me, I wanted to draw what I imagined. Working on the floor, with my paper placed on a long wooden board, I drew for days in deep concentration. It was a kind of meditation, during which my hand followed my eyes and my mind often roamed freely from one subject to another, as if separated from the activity of drawing.

Takis was busy making new works for a show at the Iris Clert Gallery. He and Raymondos returned from the forge every night, tired and blackened from the smoke and fire. We cooked our evening meal together, each having an elected skill. I decided what we would eat and how to cook the meat or vegetables, while Takis explained how things were cooked in Greece. Raymondos was a dab hand at peeling potatoes. He insisted on stocking up on them, and tinned food, believing that war might come at any time.

Takis spent evenings sitting in cafés with Minos,

mostly speaking Greek, which I did not understand. Although he professed to despise Greeks and didn't want to return to Athens, all his closest friends were Greek, including his two main dealers, Iris Clert and Alexander Iolas.

Occasionally, Takis and I would go to a bistro or take in a film. The cinemas we frequented were all on one street, near the Sorbonne. They were very small and always full. One evening, there was a commotion before the film started and we turned to see Marlene Dietrich standing at the top of the aisle with a handsome young man in tow.

Takis called his latest works *Telémagnétiques*. Nails or small sheet metal cones were tied by nylon threads to thin metal prongs projecting from metal-framed canvases or metal plates. Attracted to a magnet, they quivered in mid-air.

Takis's show opened in November and was a critical success. This upset another Iris Clert artist, Yves Klein, whose June exhibition had filled the gallery with sponges dipped in ultramarine house paint he called International Klein Blue. Takis ridiculed the blue sponges, attached with a metal rod to stones. Secretly, I liked his gold paintings, small boards covered with gold leaf, the ends loose and quivering in the slightest current of air.

I had met Klein at the Iris Clert Gallery soon after arriving in Paris, during an exhibition of his friend Jean Tinguely's drawing machines. Klein, dressed like a banker in an immaculate dark suit, white shirt and bow tie, had given a short bow and brought my hand to his mouth, before returning to more important matters. On hearing of it at the time, Jean-Jacques absolutely forbade me to meet him again: 'Klein is a member of Jeune Nation, a Fascist organization.'

Iris's relations with her artists were often intimate. Takis spent many evenings in conversation with her, and she enjoyed galvanizing her artists into action by encouraging their jealousy of each other. After *Télémagnétiques*, there was a continual exchange of information from Iris to Yves about Takis's work and then back to Takis about Yves's reaction. In this way, she fomented and stoked the fires of ambition, jealousy and enmity. She told Takis that Yves would be showing a levitating sphere at a Paris salon, without the use of string, which made Takis anxious. He believed that Klein was stealing his invention and spent sleepless nights worrying about how to protect his work. Through Minos, he contacted Alain, who still wasn't speaking to us since he was Jean-Jacques's closest friend, and, with Iris's help, persuaded him to write an article stating that Takis was the inventor of the *Télémagnétiques* sculptures. This done, Takis was somewhat relieved, but his relief didn't last long.

Iris Clert regularly consulted an astrologer and had charts done for most of her artists to see whether they would succeed. Takis's chart placed him in between Picasso and Rodin and predicted that he would have a long life. Takis asked her to have one done for me. She never showed it to me, but told us her astrologer said that, although I had a great imagination, my future did not lie in the visual arts. She thought I would succeed as a writer of romantic novels, adding that I had a diplomatic talent. She saw me as a kind of Mata Hari, a secret agent. I felt somewhat insulted but then thought the astrologer simply told Iris what she wanted to hear!

Iris was a Greek from Alexandria, as was Takis's other dealer, Alexander Iolas. Takis explained that Greeks from Egypt were more sophisticated, more refined than those from Greece or Turkey. But, with the coming of Nasser, most had had to leave, often without managing to bring their wealth with them.

Iris had been involved in the French Resistance and had been married to a Frenchman. For a while, Takis had been her lover, but the relationship didn't last because, he complained, she never stopped talking. Iris's earnings from art enabled her to live in a modern, designer-furnished apartment and to dress in the most fashionable designer clothes. Takis said that all her artists gave her their works as presents, which, instead of keeping for her own collection, she sold while their prices were still low, in order to buy Dior or Givenchy dresses or an extravagant fur coat. Iris's gallery was one small space with a glass front on to the street. She lived very much in the moment and was prepared to go to great lengths for her artists. Of course, they were all men, apart from one woman, who was not interested in the opposite sex and made sand boxes that, when tilted, created varied patterns. Iris was Queen Bee, and her hive was, in principle, for men only.

My father, hearing from me that Takis and I were living together, came to investigate. At their initial meeting Takis asked him for his consent to our marriage. My father, always difficult with my suitors, replied that, as neither of us had asked his permission to live together, he didn't see why we were asking him to condone our marriage. He knew that, since I was still only nineteen, we could not get married without his consent.

I was bubbling over with enthusiasm about Takis and Raymondos, who was working on using a pendulum to generate enough energy to pump water out of the earth. This led to years of derision from my father, who never tired of asking whether Raymondos had succeeded. Despite, or perhaps because of, my enthusiasm, my father did not warm to Takis. He advised me not to isolate myself with one man, to meet more people. He was definitely not impressed with Takis, who spoke English and French badly and didn't even have a coat. He couldn't understand the merit of Takis's work – bits of metal, floating nails. In any case, my father was not interested in art but in music and literature. He considered painting and sculpture as minor decorative adjuncts to life, not serious intellectual pursuits. But he turned up often enough, taking me to buy clothes and tempting me with his own enjoyment of luxury. He always held court in the best hotels, usually the Prince de Galles behind the Champs-Élysées, his Parisian friends, often a touch shady, dropping in for lunch or dinner. His inability to share my feelings, although predictable, cast a shadow over my still-tender relationship.

I did persuade him to buy a small yellow magnetic tableau from Takis's show and a gouache by the Dutch CoBrA artist Karel Appel from Iris Clert. Iris, who up till then had not noticed my existence, then regarded me as a person and even invited me to exhibit a small drawing at the Micro-Salon in Berlin – the first time I exhibited my work. It gave me the opportunity to show her a few of my larger *Sky Scrolls*, in the hope that she might exhibit them in her tiny gallery on the rue des Beaux Arts. She cast her eye over them briefly and told me it was impossible to sell works on paper. I began experimenting, initially trying to keep to the same imagery but on canvas instead of paper. The resist and gouache technique did not work on canvas, and I didn't think to use unprimed linen, which would have been more absorbent and might have given more interesting results.

Discovering New Materials

A bad throat infection took me to my father's home at Château Banquet in Geneva, where bed rest and antibiotics saw me through the worst. The doctor said I was very run-down and that a stay in the mountains, breathing fresh air, would help me regain my strength. My father generously paid for me to stay in a first-class hotel in Val d'Isère, where I spent the first week reading in bed or reclining on a deckchair in the sun, covered in blankets. I had been an avid reader of the Russian classics, Tolstoy and Dostoevsky, Chekov and Gogol. I loved their dark romanticism. I shared their complex desires, which I thought had been bestowed upon me by my Russian heritage. Invalided in the mountains, I felt suitably cocooned to indulge in further romantic writings of Lermontov and Thomas Mann's *Magic Mountain*. The quiet sunshine, the hush of the

snow-covered landscape and the solitary inward-
ness of time spent wandering in the imagined worlds
of great writers nourished both my body and my
mind.

Mealtimes were lonely moments. Sitting in the
large bustling dining room, windows open to the
glistening winterscape I took no part in, I surveyed
the other guests. There was one large table of muscular, athletic men and women, of similar age to me,
who were particularly lively, glowing with health,
cheeks aflame. They appeared to me such a contrast
to myself, whom I experienced as weak and pale –
although reclining in the sun must have given me a
tan. I felt envious of their energy and covetous of
their conviviality. I must have stared at them evening after evening, because after a few days one of
the women greeted me and asked whether I was
staying alone in the hotel. I discovered they were
the French Olympic team, in training for the coming
Winter Olympics. I told them I was an artist, which
raised eyebrows and even some interest, that I was
convalescing and hoped soon to do some skiing.

Over the next day or two I became especially
friendly with François, one of the male skiers. One
evening, I kept him company while he waxed his

skis. I was curious to see that he used a coloured stick that was both thin and hard, with a wick that he lit to melt the wax on to the back of his skis. He told me it was a new plastic, replacing wax, called Tefon-stift. It came in a range of colours, possibly signifying different grades of slipperiness. I noticed that the molten stuff could be extruded and stretched into thin threads of colour. I wondered whether it might replace the Crayola crayons I had been using as a resist and I asked François to give me the details of where I could obtain this new material. He gave me an assortment of his own sticks, explaining that the team had received them for free, since their approval would generate publicity. François was quiet and introverted. He didn't tell me he was one of the best skiers on the French team and was expected to be the next Olympic champion.

That night, we ended up having sex. Something, he told me, not recommended for athletes. He said that in the mountain village where he was born, one either climbed or walked downhill, life was tough, but snow changed everything. On skis, he felt as one with the mountain. He promised to teach me how to ski and, true to his word, he gave me some of his precious time to show me how to negotiate the mountain. Much later, I heard that he had come second or third that year and I felt guilty. Had I absorbed too much of his energy on that single night we spent together? I imagined myself as a vampire, sitting at my lonely table, greedily sucking up the energy of the chattering athletes by gazing at them sitting around their Olympic table.

Back in Paris, with renewed energy and enthusiasm, I began to experiment with the Tefon-stift. First, by splattering the plastic wax on to sheets of paper in constellations of small spots of colour. It was immediately apparent that this new medium would not replace the wax crayons. I realized that I had begun a new and different voyage.

In the meantime, I continued to make more scrolls. They had started out as dense cloudscapes, cloud cities floating in distant skies, but the coagulated shapes began to separate into floating creatures, dreamy sky monsters. I also made a few much smaller drawings, airborne creatures drifting in red or grey skies. It was then I felt I had come to an end. The India ink drawings were becoming stylized, almost repetitive, and I no longer travelled through them. The Tefon-stift was the path I should now take.

It was also in the shadowed rooms of rue Leopold Robert that I began to write a story as a parable. My Kafka-inspired idea was five people walking separately or sometimes in small groups towards a distant city along an interminable road. Each encountered different obstacles or attractions that prevented them from reaching the city. The people were all well known to me and, in inventing their fictitious names and destinies, I felt a sense of power.

After the luminous snow-covered mountains of Val d'Isère, I became restless and unhappy in the dingy, dark rooms of rue Leopold Robert, impatient with the everyday repetition of our lives. Flamand still came to read my Tarot and bring me wonderful books of poetry. A school friend, Suzanna Wettstein, visited me from Zurich, where she was studying architecture. Takis hardly said a word to them. He left the apartment on the ever-rarer occasions my friends visited — they did not interest him.

Then Raymondos found a room and left our company. Takis said it was a maid's room on an upper floor and that an old lady in the next room reminded Raymondos of his mother. He felt comfortable repeating his old domestic configuration.

We decided to find a better apartment. In the

Herald Tribune I found a quite spacious apartment on the ground floor of an imposing building on the Quai d'Orsay, just opposite the Place de la Concorde. We had an enormous living room, a large bedroom, a bathroom and, at the very end of a long hallway, a sparsely equipped kitchen. Apart from a couch, a large table and a couple of chairs, there was little furniture. Takis immediately pinned my *Sky Scrolls* on the walls of the hall and the living room, and furnished the living room with his *Signals*, *Magnetic Tableaux* and large bronze balls. The windows looked on to the street, and at night we could see the shimmering lights of the Concorde across the Seine.

Takis slept badly and woke early, immediately requiring coffee and a cigarette before he could face the day. He would sit in bed, back against the wall, looking blankly ahead, smoking with trembling hand. There was a prohibition on any conversation before he had his first cup of coffee. Meanwhile, I awoke alert and excited at the prospect of another day. I would make a special breakfast of eggs and toast and bring it to him on a tray but, although he raised his eyebrows in a pretence of unexpected pleasure, he could only drink the coffee.

Our friends were impressed by our new address, and we had many visitors. Minos and Alain came quite often but never once noticed my drawings, conspicuously covering the walls. I figured they wouldn't acknowledge them because they were not made by an artist they already recognized. They were not curious. They spoke only about Takis's work. Gregory Corso, the American Beat poet, was quite different. The first time he came to the apartment, he looked very carefully at the scroll pinned up in the hall. Hearing it was my work, he expressed his enthusiasm and, from then on, treated me as an artist friend, not as the girlfriend of an artist.

Apart from Takis's Greek and Parisian friends and Beat poets, there were curators, and even artists, who wanted to look at, and often acquire, a work from Takis. A willowy, carefully dressed man and his elegant wife visited, interested in buying one of Takis's works. Alfred Barr, director of the Museum of Modern Art in New York, spent time looking at *Signals*, *Spheres* and *Magnetic Tableaux*. Much to my surprise and delight, he also studied my drawings at some length, asking Takis who the artist was. He shook my hand and said, 'Congratulations, they are very fine.'

The Italian artist Lucio Fontana was particularly interested in Takis's *Spheres* and bought a large bronze. He also looked carefully at my drawings and expressed his admiration. Not long after, he exhibited several bronze spheres of his own.

One afternoon, I opened the door to a tall, sinewy man who asked whether Takis was in. When I said he wasn't, he began conversing with me intensely, as if he had quite forgotten the reason for his visit. 'I'm Sinclair,' he told me before crossing the threshold, in case, on hearing his name, I might not let him in. Once I had invited him to stay and have a coffee, he began to tell me about his research. He was conducting experiments with the tobacco mosaic virus, he told me earnestly, sitting on the edge of the couch, his body curved like a string instrument, his attention so focused on me that there was none of the distance between people who have never met before and are testing their boundaries, feeling each other out. Sinclair simply plunged in. He lived in a continuum unbroken by normal borders, unrestrained by conventions or ties. I was only too delighted by his unusual warmth and directness. I found it easy to immerse myself in his earnest conversation and I was gullible, young or open enough to take whatever he told me seriously. He was trying to create life using this virus.

I asked whether he worked in a lab, assuming he was a biologist.

'Oh no. I'm doing these important experiments in my room at the Beat Hotel. It's the perfect place for this kind of research, because I don't want other scientists to find out.'

He had come to see Takis because Takis had promised to put him into space. He, Sinclair, was going to be the first man in space! Having told me all this, he vanished.

Later, I told Takis that his scientist friend had come to see him.

'What scientist? What was his name? Oh, you mean that crazy South African poet!'

It was like opening Pandora's box, once Sinclair came into your life. He told incredible tales, but his wildest stories often had a basis in truth. There may have been a blurring of reality in some of his escapades, but, as a poet, he achieved an intense and sharply focused vision of the real.

Sinclair had a German girlfriend, an Olympic

athlete. This Amazon physically overwhelmed the reedy poet except for the day he lost his temper and raced down the narrow staircase of the Beat Hotel, a Japanese sword held high, girlfriend tumbling down the stairs, running for her life.

Sinclair felt grocers were pricing food much too high and took it upon himself to check up on them. Going from shop to shop, he jotted down in his notebook the prices of all the fruit and vegetables on display. When one shopkeeper asked what he was doing, he calmly told him that he was the food price inspector. Mostly, these stories were hearsay, and Sinclair's antics and misadventures were amusing gossip. Remembering my own experiences in his company, nothing ever seemed too outrageous for me to believe.

We visited Sinclair at the Beat Hotel, where, as one ascended the narrow staircase, it was possible to see into residents' rooms through doors left ajar, aromatic wafts of grass curling upwards, forming arabesques in the dim light. In his room, I sat on the floor cross-legged while tea was made and offered round in a shared cup, a long, thick-rolled joint passed and noisily inhaled, and I, who hardly smoked at all, coughed loudly.

I had just started to smoke Disque Bleu cigarettes, not quite as rough as Gauloises. It was much too hard to sit over a coffee at the Old Navy for any length of time without smoking. I understood Gregory, who was always restless, who couldn't sit still smoking or reading a newspaper in the Deux Magots. After a few minutes, having quickly slurped down his coffee, he would keep repeating, 'Hey, where're we going? Man, what's happening?' We discussed our very American need to do, to keep going or doing something; our feeling of impatience with the European habit of waiting around in cafés for something to happen, someone to come by and change our lives. I had felt that same impatience during my first summer in Geneva in 1955, when I was fourteen. My father's watch business was moribund, and he'd spent whole afternoons with his cronies, talking over a couple of cups of coffee. Gregory, at least, could show off by using his new battery-operated electric shaver or by jerking off under the table to shock and disgust everyone when he opened his hand full of cum. When I asked him how he became a poet, he told me that he started life as a crook, was caught stealing and put in jail, where he got hold of a dictionary and spent days reading every page: 'I fell in love with words and I became a poet.'

My father came to see our new apartment, bringing offerings he said were usually made in Russia when entering a new home. Bread and salt. His were purchased at Fouquet and came with a whole carton of pressed caviar, champagne, foie gras and chocolates. He told us that he wanted to give us a good luck token that would keep us together. He brought out a two-dollar bill and cut it in two, gave Takis one half and me the other – I still have mine.

We ate caviar for breakfast for days on end.

In February 1960, Takis and I went to New York. Because of his youthful communist affiliations, Takis had difficulties getting a visa. Due to my insistence, my father used his connections to procure one.

Takis's dealer Alexander Iolas had been buying more of Takis's sculptures to help him make work for a solo exhibition in New York, at his gallery on the ground floor of a spacious town house at 123 East 55th Street. Iolas lived on the floors above, with his sister, Niki, and her American husband. I helped Takis make the new works in New York, in a small basement studio on West 4th Street that we borrowed from a South American artist, with whom I later traded work.

Takis and I stayed in a run-down rooming house and shared a small kitchen full of cockroaches. We hardly ever cooked there, eating mostly in Greek luncheonettes, where Takis would get friendly with the waiters, calling them compatriots and speaking Greek. I took Takis to meet my grandmother, whom I hadn't seen for two years. She had fully recovered from an earlier stroke and was living with her German-American boyfriend and ex-tenant, Mr Peck, in our old apartment on West 94th Street.

In our spare time, we went to Times Square movies, taking in double-feature gangster films in one cinema and then moving to the next one for another double feature. We loved these B-rated movies, many of which were gangster biopics. *Baby Face Nelson*, *Machine-Gun Kelly* and *Al Capone* would become cult films a decade later.

I met the novelist Iris Owens at the White Horse Tavern, and she introduced me to William Burroughs – a very thin man in a grey suit, shirt, tie and homburg hat. Iris said he tried to blend in, to make himself invisible. When I first met him, he was polite but reserved, saying very little.

We discovered Canal Street, where it was possible to find all kinds of ex-army materials. Rummaging through the wares in open crates on the sidewalk, Takis bought things for immediate use, and I chose a few curious objects that I felt might inspire me to develop my work. Some of my objects inevitably found their way into Takis's works. He bought me a bracelet made of a solid steel ring, no doubt formerly a part of a machine. I wore it to his opening and, on passing one of the larger works, my arm was clamped tight to its bullhorn-shaped magnet.

Iolas liked me because I had no airs and, as he said to Takis, I looked like a boy. During this exhibition we noticed that Iolas kept several valuable paintings stacked next to the toilet in the small gallery bathroom alongside two of Takis's early iron figures, loosely wrapped in newsprint. Takis told me he had seen a Dalí drawing and urged me to steal it – no one would notice. I told him that if he wanted to take it, he should do the job himself.

I had long hair and never quite knew what to do with it. Brooks, Iolas's partner, recommended a hairdresser to whom I went on the afternoon before the opening. That evening, I felt very stylish with my new hairdo, wearing an expensive dress my father had bought me in Paris. Dalí's agent asked if I would agree to model Dalí's jewellery. I was thrilled but made the mistake of telling Takis, who discouraged me, much like my father had when I'd been offered a job in Paris modelling hats. Takis said why would I waste my time modelling Dalí's rubbish jewellery – I should know that he had sold out long ago and wasn't making anything worth looking at any more.

During the show set-up, Iolas had said some mean things; something about how he couldn't bear clever women. The day after the opening he came into the gallery with a present of a small, cute white dog, half chihuahua, half fox terrier. He said he'd won it at a lottery and that it reminded him of me. Why? Perhaps Takis did treat me like his sexy pet, looking up to him with adoring eyes and wagging tail, following him without question. And Takis did have an animal nickname for me, a Greek endearment – not a dog but a deer.

I named the dog Kukla and took her on a German boat back to France, enjoying a smooth, sunny crossing. In Paris, Kukla received a lot of attention. She was a beautiful, intelligent dog, with large dark eyes and a smooth coat. We had a lot of trouble house-training her, Takis with his theories and me with mine, but we loved her dearly and were overcome with grief when she was run over one day as she raced after us through the large *porte cochère*, left ajar. Takis and I wept over her small limp body and found a secluded grove in the Bois de Boulogne where we could bury her. Takis said she was too pure and special to live, and her soul would transmigrate to a higher level.

In spring 1960, I decided to learn to drive. The only car I wanted was the Triumph TR3, a beautifully designed sports car, low and curvaceous. It had to be British racing green with a light grey leather interior. I was not normally acquisitive and owning material things had never been high on my wish list, but every now and again I had a sudden desire for a very precise object. In pursuit of my objective, I took lessons. My irascible instructor chose the incredibly difficult and frightening Place de la Concorde to inculcate me with the arcane French system of *priorité à droite* ('right have priority'). An avalanche of cars circled the Concorde and I hesitated to move forward. He compounded my fear by shouting, 'Allez, allez-y. Vous avez la priorité! Allez-y, mon Dieu! Rappelez-vous la priorité à droite' ('Go on, go on. You have right of way! Go on, for God's sake! Remember your right of way'). And I would inch my way forward, expecting to be crushed by the onslaught of fast-approaching cars. To my amazement, they all came to a halt, allowing me the promised right of way.

When it came to the driving test, I was suitably inured and trained. I was also extremely lucky, in that my examiner had the opposite character to my instructor. He was delighted to examine a young American woman because he was learning English, and this was an opportunity to practise. Increasing my anxiety, all his commands were given in a decidedly broken, often incomprehensible English. However, he ignored my mistakes and when it was all over, and I expected to fail, he congratulated me in English: 'You make good driving, Mademoiselle!'

I flew to visit my father, hoping to persuade him to buy me my dream car. He was not at all content with my choice and countered that the Triumph Herald was a nice car for a young lady. I thought it was very bourgeois and not at all my style – and I was horrified by the idea of myself as a young lady. He took me to the garage where he'd bought his vast cream Chrysler convertible to look at the Herald. I didn't like it.

The next afternoon, over lunch with some friends of his, he suggested we all go to Divonne on Saturday night for dinner. He meant dinner at the Casino restaurant.

I refused to go, saying I didn't want to watch him gambling.

'We'll just go for dinner. I won't gamble.'

'You always say that, but I know you will.'

He put on his most charming expression, intense light blue eyes twinkling in his heavily lined face. 'But you bring me luck.'

That was my chance and I jumped. 'If I do and you win, will you buy me the TR3? If you promise, I'll come along.'

My father looked resignedly at his friends. 'I've been tricked by my own daughter.'

We drove to Divonne quite early and, as promised, sat down for dinner, after which my father casually said he'd go to the gaming room for a moment, to see who was playing. He meant at chemin de fer, his favourite game of chance. I followed him, noting that he didn't buy any chips but approached the table and observed the game for a while. Then, when a seat became free, he sat down and gestured to one of the attendants, who immediately brought him a stack of chips. I guessed he was playing on credit. My father's moment stretched to hours. He started by losing most of the large chips he had been given, asked for more and then slowly began to win. In chemin de fer, the bank travels around the table from player to player. Once a player becomes banker, they have a statistical advantage and, if they win, can keep their bank growing and continue playing or pass and take their winnings. The winning player is the one whose hand comes closest to the number seven. My father's bank grew and grew as his lucky streak continued. It was exciting to watch him win, but then I began to feel nervous that his whole pile would be swept away when someone came up with better cards and declared *Banco*.

It was by now four in the morning, and the other players were leaving the table. There was an atmosphere of dejection hanging heavily with the pall of cigarette smoke that enveloped them all. My father had been playing all night and, even if he wasn't, I was exhausted from the tension and the hours of sitting in the suffocating atmosphere under the grim lights.

I elbowed him. 'Let's go. You've won so much, don't lose it.'

'I can't leave yet. I must give the players who lost a chance to win their money back.'

My father's luck turned, but he stayed on, giving back some of his winnings to those who remained, determined to claw back what they'd lost. When we finally left the Casino, the sun was rising. He had won about 30,000 francs. My father looked at the sunrise and said, 'Isn't life beautiful.'

True to his word, we went to his garage to see whether they could order a TR3 in British racing green with a light grey interior. He still tried to change my mind but, seeing I was determined, ordered the TR3. It arrived a week later and a young mechanic from the garage had to show me how to drive it. I was a little nervous, seeing as it was my first car and that it roared when my foot pressed the gas pedal, even lightly. Once I'd learned to double clutch to shift into reverse, my father decided that he wanted to drive, to show me how it was done. He was used to driving an automatic and would forget to change gear, or do so without using the clutch, and the car would screech with pain. I sat there, tense and unhappy, imagining he was ruining my new car but unable to say a word since he'd had the grace to buy it for me.

Summer of Sadness

JULY 1960

It was 13 July when I read the inconspicuous announcement. I was still in Geneva, making ready to go to bed with a book. By chance, I had picked up a copy of the *Herald Tribune*. My eyes were drawn by the name, her name: Nina.

L.A. CITY COLLEGE COED STRANGLED

Nina Thoeren, daughter of Robert Thoeren, the
Hollywood scriptwriter, was strangled to death
last night on her way home from the library.
Police, called to the scene of the crime by residents
alerted by the sound of screams, arrived too late to
revive her. They arrested R. W. Clemmons of
2030 2nd Avenue.

Was it Nina? How could that have happened to her of all people? The immediacy of horror, the neutrality of its delivery. I couldn't take it in. It was so completely unreal. Nina in Los Angeles studying biology, late at the college library, on her way home to her apartment, I didn't know where. I had never been to Los Angeles, so couldn't imagine it.

A car stopping and a black face offering her a ride. How could she refuse? Once in the car, he said she taunted him. It was his word. No one could gainsay it. There was no one. She asked him what he did, and when he told her he was a door-to-door Bible salesman, she asked him if he didn't have a ball in his glove compartment and made to open it. There'd been a spate of sex crimes and the press had called the assailant the bouncing ball murderer. When he stopped at a red light, she opened the car door and jumped out, running for nearby apartment blocks. He caught up with her, pushed her screaming against a wall and, too frightened, he strangled her. People didn't come out of their nearby houses. They called the police, but when they arrived he was standing over her and Nina was dead.

I had lost my close friend. My only solace was that we had met again before she left Paris and we had parted as friends. I remembered the drawing of the rapist that Nina had bought from Minos;

I shuddered as I saw once again the masked man pointing the gun at her, me, you, at all women. And in the barrel of his gun, the image of a naked girl.

Sadly, life moves on.

Takis flew to Geneva and, after a couple of tense days with my father, I drove my new racing-green TR3 over the Simplon Pass into Italy, to Venice. I was a beginner, driving a sports car over narrow mountainous roads with sharp curves and steep cliff edges. This was before the Swiss built motorways across the Alps, before the Mont Blanc tunnel. Takis, who didn't drive, hung his head out of the window and called out how much space I had before the road dropped away. It was frightening, but I was determined to stay alive.

We lodged once again at Locanda Montin in the Dorsoduro, near the Accademia with its wondrous arched wooden bridge, standing at the top of which, one moonlit night a lifetime ago, Nina had spoken to me so dramatically about Venice as a devourer of men. She was still so present in my thoughts and dreams, but I knew I would never see her again. I both wanted to and dreaded visiting Manina, who I knew would be suffering the unbelievable, unacceptable loss of her beautiful daughter. I imagined that seeing me – young, alive and well, with whom her daughter had shared so many experiences – would deepen her pain. On our first day in Venice, Takis and I went to see her.

Manina spoke of Nina's appointment with fate. She had tried to keep her from leaving Europe, but Nina's uncle, who was executor of her father's estate, disapproved of Manina and disapproved of Nina living with artists in Paris. He'd told Nina that he would no longer fund her dissolute Parisian life. Manina believed that he'd wanted to put as much distance between Nina and herself as possible, thus the choice of California. Now she would have to go there to plead for the murderer's life. Nina would not have wished for this man to be put on the electric chair. She abhorred capital punishment.

Manina lovingly looked after her bedridden mother, whose severe osteoporosis had kept her supine for over ten years. Manina told us that to tell her mother about Nina's death would surely kill her. Nina had written frequently, long letters from Los Angeles that now she herself would have to continue. Surely, that would be torture. We hugged her, we wept together, and I felt guilty for being alive.

*

One morning, soon after our arrival, I woke to find I was alone in bed. I could hear three voices and laughter drifting up from the garden; one belonged to Takis, one was a woman. I had the uncomfortable feeling that Venice, once imbued with a supreme sense of happiness, the joy of meeting an old friend again, the glow of mutual friendship and new love, the welcome of complete acceptance, was about to show me a different and uneasy face. I felt oddly alone and abandoned. Dressing hurriedly, I went down to the covered garden, where breakfast was served. Takis was happily chatting with a young woman and an older man. Without being introduced, I sat down.

Then Takis explained: 'You were sleeping and I didn't want to wake you, so I came down for a coffee. These two were already here. Alan brought this beautiful girl to meet me. He says she is also a genius.'

The girl interrupted. 'Hi. I'm Amy Mims. I'm an Irish revolutionary.' And turning to Alan, who was gazing at her with admiration, 'So, to continue, I'm now working on an epic poem, *Daedalus*, that will be derived from both Greek and Irish mythology. Of course, you know the Irish came originally from Greece and brought the Greek poetic tradition with them. There is also a possibility that they were the Lost Tribe of Israel, but I prefer to think of them as Greeks, wouldn't you?'

Takis smoked and listened, leaning back in his chair and examining Amy with amusement. Alan explained who she was. 'Amy just graduated from Harvard, *cum laude*. She is not only one of the first women to do so but also, at eighteen, the youngest. Her subject is European literature with an emphasis on Greece and Ireland. She is fluent in Ancient Greek and speaks six languages.'

Alan Ansen, a flamboyant American poet and playwright, a great friend of Gregory Corso, William Burroughs and Allen Ginsberg, lived in Venice and Athens. He was himself a Greek scholar who had graduated from Harvard. He was a portly man, with a large head, intelligent, thoughtful eyes and an open, welcoming demeanour.

Amy was taking full advantage of all the attention. She had shoulder-length auburn hair that she tossed as a horse would its mane. Her face, although pretty, had a coarse feel that I happily decided would increase with years. She wore a long, full, gypsy skirt and a light blouse that slipped off her shoulders as she waved her arms. She exuded a wild energy that made me feel tame and uninteresting. This was the beginning of my struggle with recurrent painful feelings of jealousy and inadequacy. From the comfortable security of being daddy's favourite girl, I was catapulted into the disturbing reality of being one of many, all fighting for attention and love.

The remainder of our stay I spent learning how to drink Martinis in Alan's apartment, feeling dreamy, sensual and torpid, overcome by the heat and odours of Venice, the food sizzling, baking, simmering in the trattorias, the dank smell from the ubiquitous waterways blending with traces of perfumed suntan lotion from the crowd slowly moving down the beaten paths through the city.

Caresse Crosby and the Castello di Rocca Sinibalda

Caresse Crosby had first met Takis in Greece when he was twenty-seven, and helped him leave Athens to live in Paris. Hers was a long history of patronage of the arts. She was a free spirit born into an old colonial American family. She invented the brassiere in 1913, aged twenty-one. She tried and failed to make and sell her bras as a business, so she sold the patent to Warner Brothers for $1,500.

In the 1920s, she divorced her first husband and married Harry Crosby, a nephew of the banker J. P. Morgan. They founded the Black Sun Press and published the early work of such authors as T. S. Eliot, James Joyce, Henry Miller and Anaïs Nin.

Caresse and Gary Davis initiated Citizens of the World, with the support of her friend Buckminster Fuller. They burned their passports and travelled without them, often being thrown into jail. She also founded Women for Peace, visiting Gandhi and other sympathetic world leaders.

Caresse bought the Castello di Rocca Sinibalda a few years before we visited in early August 1960. I remember hearing that she'd paid $10,000 for over a hundred rooms, some huge with twenty-foot ceilings, frescoed salons with sixteenth-century furniture. She had rented it from the Vatican for a summer in the 1950s, so she was familiar with its ruined state and scorpion inhabitants. The castle came with the title of Principessa, and Caresse was known by that title in the village nestled at its foot. She spent her summers there and invited paying guests. Her non-paying guests were artists, painters, poets, photographers and musicians. They seemed to be in such a majority that I wondered how she afforded her generous hospitality.

She invited us to visit her after Venice, and we stayed with her for at least a month, having driven there in my Triumph with the roof down, my skill slowly improving over the long journey. The castle was 70 kilometres north of Rome, on the old Flaminia road, over which I drove several times during our stay. An Italian racing driver was visiting for a few days and, impressed by my new car, gave me supplementary driving lessons. The area was ideal because it was all sharp curves and narrow mountainous roads. He taught me that it was best to brake before going into a curve but to accelerate once in it. One of those handy bits of advice one never forgets.

Takis and I had a large room, bare except for a bed and a big wooden cupboard. Every night we lay in bed inspecting the ceiling for scorpions and, if Takis saw one, he would ask me to kill it. He couldn't, he claimed, because he was born under their star sign. I was worried that one might drop on us during the night, and with the ceiling being over twenty feet high, they were very difficult to kill.

We got into the healthy morning habit of climbing the staircase (our room was on the entry floor) and taking the winding narrow steps up to the castle ramparts that were wide enough to allow me to do the yoga asanas I had learned in Paris. Up there, where we thought no one could see us, Takis sunbathed naked, while I, also naked, exercised. My father had given me a camera and Takis suggested we photograph each other in erotic poses.

Caresse's old friend Elsa Schiaparelli came for a

brief stay. Upright and formal, she had a sense of humour and a sharp mind, as I discovered when we played charades to while away the long evenings. Roloff Beny, a Canadian artist and photographer and a friend of Peggy Guggenheim, gave us a copy of his wonderful book on India after a weekend stay. Alan Ansen visited and mentioned that he had seen me doing yoga on the ramparts, adding how beautiful I looked in those asanas. In addition to all these visitors, there was an introverted American painter who seemed to be in permanent residence in a small room at the very top of the castle. Caresse asked the permanent inhabitants to help out with restorations.

The castle was built between 1530 and 1560, and it was said that the original plans were drawn by Leonardo da Vinci. It was in the shape of a huge bird, and the tail was a large hanging garden where we had drinks at sunset, often remaining there for dinner. After dinner, we retired to Caresse's intimate salon, well furnished and decorated with paintings and photographs given to her by famous artists like Salvador Dalí and Max Ernst. Caresse was very strict about dressing for dinner and, to please her, we would change into somewhat more presentable attire. We often played cinema charades after dinner, and Takis and I were always on opposite teams. I had the feeling that he was completely at sea and his team mostly lost. When we were alone, he asked me how we had won. 'Tell me, you cheated,' he insisted, unable to accept losing, except in a crooked game. Of course, we hadn't cheated. I was articulate and acting came very easily. Not that I liked games. I didn't like competing, being put in a position of winning or losing, the former embarrassing, the latter painful. But cinema charades were different, more of a team effort. Takis was unable to play almost any game. If he couldn't win, he wasn't interested.

My hair had grown very long and I almost always pinned it up in a braided chignon. I decided it was time for a change. Roloff gave me the name of a hairdresser in Rome, who transformed my appearance. The short, asymmetrical 1920s style with a bang on one side made me feel more boyish and adventurous. I drove back at night on my own, feeling quite glamorous and new. The cut was a success and Takis photographed me to celebrate it.

I had brought rolls of paper, wax crayons, pen and ink, and spent time painting in our large, silent room, or in one of the many empty rooms. The light was quite different to Parisian light, altering the look of my drawings. I showed them to Caresse, who responded with positive, encouraging remarks. We had long talks, during which she reminisced about her youth and her years in Paris with her husband; how free they had felt but how freedom became excess, ending with his horrible suicide. That morning they had stood together on the balcony of their suite at the Waldorf, and Harry told her he didn't want to grow old. He asked her to jump with him, while they were happy and in love, but she refused. He killed himself with another woman that same day, leaving her alone to suffer the pain of losing him and to deal with the scandal of the double suicide. Caresse confided that her way of handling this was to plunge into a whirl of relationships with many other men. Behaviour that neither family nor friends understood. Caresse was seventy that summer, with cataracts in both eyes. She wore heavy, thick glasses but always dressed elegantly and carried herself with self-assurance. She was the first older woman to speak to me as an equal, and I felt privileged to be treated as her friend.

Takis and I went to Rome. We tried to visit the

Vatican Museum but were turned away three times for not wearing the right clothes. Each time something was wrong that they'd not mentioned the last time. I couldn't wear shorts or trousers and had to cover my head. We gave up, swearing against the Pope and all his treasures. In the Colosseum, Takis embraced me. We were promptly admonished by a lurking policeman, who told us we could be fined for kissing in public. The early sixties were not yet swinging in Rome.

We met Suna Portman and her American boyfriend, Bill Barker, beautiful blonds who displayed cool detachment. Suna's pouting Bardot lips declared to all that she was on laxatives and had to stay close to a toilet. Her sixteen-year-old brother, Mikey, became attached to William Burroughs and sank into a fatally destructive heroin habit. William managed his own habit, but Mikey was too young. Suna and Bill came to Rocca, where they lounged about, looking the height of fashion no matter how they dressed. Takis thought I behaved badly towards them, that I was jealous of Suna, which I might well have been, and made me feel guilty about my negative emotions. To expiate these, I made Suna a sacrificial offering of an enormous transistor radio my father had given me. He had switched from exporting watches to being an agent for the Japanese company Standard. He loved novelty and invention and came into the business at the very beginning of the transistor revolution. I was attached to this radio, but guilt was deeply engrained in my psyche. My mother had always labelled me as jealous, greedy and stingy – *Eifersüchtig!* If I accepted that I felt envious of Suna's golden hair, tall, willowy body or incredible self-possession, I had to counter it with an equivalent gesture, as in an algebraic equation. One could discuss at length the symbolism of the sacrifice, but Suna was puzzled and pleased to receive such a gift. After which, I became, as with Iris Clert, more noticeable.

We discovered a clear, cold stream at the foot of the castle that came from the nearby Apennines, deserted except for the women who went there to wash their laundry and a few boys fishing. From the castle the stream was only a shimmering serpentine line of light, so we thought no one would notice if we went skinny-dipping. Takis and I, Suna and Bill descended to bathe in the cool water, sunbathe on the boulders and share the occasional joint, unaware we were being watched by some of the village boys – two of whom I met as adults many years later in Umbria.

Perhaps because his own emotions were so intense, Takis advised me that emotions were poison and should, at all costs, be eradicated. Takis enjoyed the role of guru. He recalled an encounter with the followers of the Russian mystic philosopher Gurdjieff. Albert Gilou, art collector and founder and arts editor of *Connaissance des Arts*, asked Takis to describe the most transformative event in his life. When Takis replied, 'seeing a solar eclipse', Gilou declared that Takis was a reincarnation of Gurdjieff. After this, Gurdjieff's followers were very helpful to Takis, one collector buying his works and then returning them for him to sell again. Takis respected Gurdjieff's teachings and told me to read P. D. Ouspensky's *In Search of the Miraculous*. He taught that most humans do not possess a unified consciousness, and thus live their lives in a state of hypnotic 'waking sleep', but that it is possible to transcend to a higher state of consciousness and achieve full human potential.

Takis complained he was losing his hair, which, very fine in texture, was becoming thinner and thinner. I suggested that he shave it all off because it would grow back revitalized. Once he'd shaved his head, Takis did physically resemble the 'great master'.

We sometimes went to see films in the small, dusty town of Rieti. The cinema was in a room normally dedicated to other activities. It had a large screen at one end with rows of simple upright wooden chairs and benches. The locals, mainly men and teenage boys, filled the room, smoking and waiting noisily for the film to begin. There was always a newsreel, glowing footage of government ministers accompanied by important heads of state, princes, queens, film stars or athletic heroes in glamorous attire and expensive cars. The locals were meant to experience vicariously the unreachable wealth, the importance and good fortune of the more privileged. All the films were dubbed into Italian because so many people were illiterate. This proved disastrous as far as we were concerned, since Gregory Peck wasn't Gregory Peck when a completely unrecognizable voice spoke Italian. The only actors who sounded just as funny, or even funnier, were Laurel and Hardy. I heard that they took the trouble to dub their own films into Italian with their very own English accents.

*

Towards the end of August, Takis and I decided that it would be good for me to spend some time on my own. I would take him to Rome airport and continue alone by car to Athens. Takis wanted me to restore his old studio in Anakasa. He gave me detailed instructions about how to find it, whom to approach for building materials and whom to ask to do the work. I was to meet his youngest sister, Tita, who would help me. Once the studio was restored, I could live and make my own work there for a month. As Takis said, 'To make your own experiences.'

Caresse suggested we meet in Delphi sometime in late September. She was trying to establish a Centre for World Peace and had chosen Delphi because the ancient Greeks believed that it was the *omphalos*, or 'navel', of the world.

Discovering Greece

SEPTEMBER 1960

I enjoyed the long drive to Athens in a fast car with a breeze caressing my face; it gave me a sense of freedom. I realized that I enjoyed being on my own, stopping when and where I wanted, on the spur of the moment, without discussion or explanation. Since my destination was the Brindisi ferry, I drove to Naples and crossed through Campania to Bari. I felt deeply moved by the landscape, at this time of year ochre dry, the endless groves of ancient olive trees dancing past me in a fluttering of grey-green leaves. Along the sea were large walled properties that I longed to explore. It was a land imbued with memory, a deep sense of innumerable lives.

On the boat, two Greek men asked me where I was heading and, when I told them Athens, offered to serve as my guides. That turned out to be a piece of luck. Immediately on landing there was a real change in the appearance of things, due to the quality of light. Everything appeared in sharper contrast. On the way to Ioannina, I spotted a large brown bag lying in the middle of the road and drove over it. There was a terrible thud and the car stopped. The bag turned out to be a hard rock. My guides organized a temporary repair that would take me to Athens, where I could get the car properly looked at.

I missed Takis, his warmth and company, but being on my own was also liberating. Although I suffered dark moments of loneliness and despair, when what I had promised Takis I would do went badly wrong, the sadness I felt due to our separation did not last.

Athens was a small town, appearing to sleep on in layers of dust. The streets had an unused feeling with old, ponderous cars passing now and then. I had fantasized Athens as an ancient Greek city — not just the surviving monuments, like the Acropolis and archaeological ruins, but the houses people lived in. Takis had told me that when he was a boy, Athens was full of old romantic villas, but they'd gradually been replaced with cheaply built apartment buildings in the European style.

On my first day, I walked to a large café with little marble tables spread out across the sidewalk. Men, predominantly older men, sat in small groups, playing backgammon, watching intently, smoking, absently swinging their *komboloi* (worry beads) or fingering them carefully. Not a woman in sight, they didn't go to cafés – didn't want to, weren't meant to or hadn't the time. Whereas men seemed to have all the time in the world. I approached in my shorts and T-shirt and, politely, they appeared barely to notice me. I wanted to order something entirely Greek and chose *mastika*,* which the waiter seemed to think I would like. He brought a glass of cold water and a small plate on which rested a tea-spoonful of something white and sticky. I asked what I was meant to do. He mimed placing the *mastika*-filled spoon in the water and then in my mouth.

I chose a cheap hotel on Aiolou Street in Monastiraki, the district of the Athens flea market. It was very basic and so near the Acropolis that I could see part of it through my window. On my return one evening, I thought my bed had been slept in, and

* *Mastika* is a Greek sweet made from a natural tree resin.

someone had gone through my belongings. Nothing was missing. Later, someone told me that those cheap hotels rented out already taken rooms, for an hour at a time, to prostitutes or couples looking for a place to make love.

Takis had told me many stories about Athenian life and had written in my notebook various hints, the main places to visit and the names and addresses of people who would be helpful to restore the studio:

- his mother, Kuria Vassilaki, her address and roughly where that was
- special cafés, such as the Brazilian, next to the Pallas cinema, where the intellectual elite of Athens would congregate from one to two o'clock in the afternoon; and the Byzantion, where interesting people went from midnight till two in the morning
- the olives best for blood were bitter, called *thrubes*
- the salad good for your skin was *rathikia italica*. Refined olive oil was better
- the best sections of Attica were north, north-west, west

I was to ask his sister Tita to introduce me to his good friend Manolis, who would help me to restore his studio. In Terma Patissia, where his mother lived, there was a building supplies store, Madra. I was to tell the director that I was a friend of Takis, who sent him his regards, and that I planned to rebuild his studio. Could he recommend two builders, two men he guaranteed would work well and be honest, and I would buy all my materials from him, if he gave me a good discount.

Takis drew a small street plan and wrote the Greek alphabet in my notebook, with a few phrases to start me off.

The day after I arrived, I decided to visit Takis's mother, Kuria Vassilaki. My car was a complete novelty in Athens. Cars were few, and I didn't see one other sports car. I looked at my map, but it was hard to read the scarce street signs, so I stopped a pedestrian and, in my best Greek, asked him the way:

'Pou eine Terma Patision Sinikismos Prombona?'

He rattled off directions in Greek, but I didn't understand a word. He mimed that he would accompany me there, got into my car and took me to her door. On the way, he explained that he thought I spoke Greek, since my accent was so good. Takis had not given me his mother's precise address, just the name of the road and the general neighbourhood, but he had described the house so vividly that I immediately recognized its broken-down gate and garden bare of all but weeds and a couple of fig trees. The property was adjacent to a large, enclosed garden, also described by Takis, inside which was the Garden of Paradise taverna. I knocked on the gate and a small, emaciated figure, wearing a colourless smock and oversized slippers, shuffled across the dusty yard. I knew this was Krystallo, his mother's ancient servant, who, since being taken in by Kuria Vassilaki during the German occupation, was her willing slave, working for almost nothing.

Krystallo was born on a mountainous island. Her family didn't send her to school; instead she did menial chores and looked after sheep. At fourteen she became pregnant and, terrified of the consequences, told no one, gave birth to the baby alone, out with her sheep, and left it in the wild, hoping it would die. The baby did die, but the tiny body was discovered by another shepherd and brought to the village. Krystallo could not hide her crime and, rejected by her family, was thrown into prison. The villagers threatened to stone her to death, forcing the authorities to transfer her to the mainland. The magistrate took pity on the young illiterate girl, since she was docile and repentant. She was released and a family was found in Athens for whom she could work as a servant in exchange for food and board. Takis said she was the purest soul because her ego had been burned to nothing by her sufferings, because she considered herself a worthless criminal who deserved nothing. When the Germans invaded Greece, her employers, for whom she had by then worked for around five years, earning nothing but leftovers and rags, decided she was one too many to feed and sent her away. Krystallo had never been out of the house on her own and had no idea where to go or what to do. She sat down on a street corner and waited to die. Kuria Vassilaki happened to be passing and asked the despondent girl what she was doing there. Hearing her story, Kuria Vassilaki took her home, where she was very unwelcome since the family had little enough to eat. The family consisted of Kuria Vassilaki's six remaining children, Giorgos, Vassilis, Takis, and three girls, Lilika, Titika and Tita. Her eldest and, according to Takis, most gifted son, had starved himself to death at news of the impending Nazi occupation.

During the winter famine of 1941–2, the family survived on soup made from re-boiling raisins sent to them by relatives in the Peloponnese. Krystallo, guilty about partaking in their meagre rations, secretly collected snails and ate them, swelling up like a balloon. Dangerously ill, she was taken to hospital, where she was given food and soon recovered.

Takis's father had been an affluent landowner on the Attica plain north of Athens. In 1928, Greek refugees from Turkey settled like a swarm of locusts on his land. He spent much of his capital trying to obtain the return of his unfairly state-requisitioned land. When that proved impossible, he spent the rest on opening a taverna with a close relation. Unfortunately, he did not have a head for business and, without the land, was unable to survive. He died before the Italian invasion, deeply depressed by his inability to regain his fortune, or even make a decent living.

Takis's mother continued as if nothing had changed. A woman of great dignity, head held high, she defied her still-wealthy cousins. She never let anyone forget that, during the First World War, she had earned a medal for her heroism as a nurse on the battlefield, a medal pinned on her by the Greek Queen.

Two years later, when sitting around an embroidered-cloth-covered table as Krystallo brought out lunch, one fork at a time, Takis, surveying the dust and assorted garbage in her front yard, said, 'You used to be a woman of means, Mother. This was once a villa with a garden full of flowers.'

She replied, 'Yes. The rings have fallen, but the fingers are still there.'

Krystallo led me across the yard, where a goat was tethered to a fig tree, past the garage, its door propped up against a wall, and I remembered Takis's story about his brother Vassilis, who raced cars and was very lazy. He wouldn't bother to get out of his car, but simply drove through the door to garage it. As Krystallo opened the door to the house, a large dog nearly knocked her over, and she cried out in a crackling voice for it to stay down and ushered me in. The hallway was dark and cool, and the wide back of Kuria Vassilaki was bent over a telephone into which she was speaking loudly. Krystallo left me there, returning to her kitchen. When she'd finished her call, Kuria Vassilaki turned around and greeted me warmly. She had a broad, open face, with large, dark eyes and a strong, straight nose. Apart from her abundant grey hair, treated with a violet rinse popular in Athens at the time, she greatly resembled Takis, although, unlike him, she was very overweight.

She spoke quite rapidly in Greek and, although I only understood a few words, I felt I understood everything. I felt at home, very comfortable with this warm, larger-than-life lady whose daughter Tita would join us shortly. She loved using her phone to talk with family and friends, but it had been out of order. Takis had sent her the money to get it working again, which made her very happy. Apart from this treasure, her house lacked all modern comforts.

For my first visit to Takis's studio in Anakasa, I went with Manolis and Tita, who spoke some English and acted as translator and guide. The one-room shack was perched on the edge of a narrow ravine through which trains passed regularly with an ear-splitting roar, a tremor shaking the flimsy, cement-block walls. Anakasa was a collection of illegally built houses. Building without a permit was illegal, but to obtain a building permit one had to own a certain amount of land. The only way around the restriction was to put up a roofed structure in one night. Some successful attempts had slowly expanded from one-room shacks to proper homes. No house had running water, and all the villagers got their water from one communal outdoor tap at the entrance to the village, where women stood and gossiped by the side of the road. Electricity was obtained illegally by connecting to the nearest electric pole, so that wires stretched from house to house. When Manolis pushed open the door, I was struck by the poverty of the interior and the mystery emanating from two plaster figures, standing like archaic totems guarding the space. There was no furniture, apart from a wooden table on which stood an unfinished plaster head and a few tools. It looked very much as if the room had been broken into and whatever else it had contained taken away.

Manolis said that Takis had asked him to look after the studio and he had come from time to time. Sadly, it had been vandalized, the door smashed in, but, as I could see, he had repaired it and put on a padlock. Some things had been taken, mainly old furniture and a stove, but the sculptures were intact.

I asked him about restoring it so that I could live there, and he promised he would help. Unfortunately, Manolis did not turn out to be an honest friend.

Takis had given me some money to repair the studio. Manolis insisted that he would be able to buy materials much cheaper than I could and asked for money in advance to pay the builders. I was too young and naive, and Manolis disappeared with the cash. No work was done that summer. I visited the studio again and again, hoping that he would come as promised. On one visit, I made friends with a woman who lived in Anakasa, using much sign language and a few Greek words that I'd picked up quickly. Kuria Nitza showed me how to cook a Greek stew and how to tell whether someone had been struck by the evil eye, a superstition much believed in. I felt a bit unwell, and she offered to see whether someone might have given me the evil eye. She took a bowl of water and carefully tipped in a few drops of olive oil, which does not normally dissolve in water, but, as she enthusiastically demonstrated, when the evil eye was present it did.

Whenever I went to a café or a taverna, I was always the only woman, and my meal was usually paid for before I could pay. The same thing happened when I tried to go to a cinema in Tripolis, in the Peloponnese. I was standing in a line of men and, when my turn came to pay, the lady behind the till waved me forward. When I showed her my money, she motioned to a man, and he simply nodded. I was never approached or pestered. I frequented popular places in Omonia or Monastiraki but had not yet been to Kolonaki, which Takis had told me to avoid. In Monastiraki I found old 78 rpm hard plastic records of authentic bazouki and zimbekiko, which I bought for a few drachmas. I visited the museums and the Acropolis and drove to Sounion to see the magnificent temple of Poseidon, facing the infinite sea and sky.

On one drive back to Monastiraki from Anakasa, I took a wrong turn and became completely lost on dusty dirt roads. I stopped the TR3 and was immediately surrounded by a posse of small boys, emerging from clouds of white dust. I tried asking directions, but their only interest was where I came from. Then another car appeared. Two German men in their twenties saw I was lost, asked me where I was going and offered to show me the way to my hotel. Back in central Athens, they asked if I would like to have dinner with them at a seafront restaurant. We drove in my car quite far along the coast. The atmosphere in the restaurant reminded me of a dimly lit jazz club in Paris, with music, men and women sitting together, eating and drinking. The young Germans openly shared a joint with me. Then one began to talk about what it must be like to kill someone. Alarm bells began to ring as he continued wondering aloud, as if it were the most natural thing in the world to discuss. I realized that I was alone with these men, far from Athens, in a place I didn't know. The only thing in my favour was that I had insisted on using my own car. Choosing my moment, I said I was tired and wanted to drive back and perhaps they would like to stay on as it was still early. But they insisted on accompanying me back to my hotel. I drove but felt frightened the whole way, although there was no more mention of knives and killing. I didn't want to see them again. Subsequently, someone told me those Germans were drug dealers.

There were very few tourists in Athens and all the ancient sites, including the Acropolis, were freely accessible. I often wandered alone through the ancient remains. Restoration work was being done, and I was fascinated by the sound of wind in the scaffolding.

> I heard music unlike I had ever heard. Timeless, it seemed to come from the Parthenon itself . . . It was magical – sky music – vibrations – then I realised it was the wind flowing through the metal tubes of the scaffolding. Magic music – nature creates it within the mechanical makings of man, but he himself does not hear . . . or see the poetry of their own modern devices.

I decided to visit the island of Hydra. On the ferry, I met a young Greek who spoke a bit of English and invited me to see Aegina, the island before Hydra. He said there would be a large full moon and he could take me to see the temple of Aphaia, on the other side of the island, in the moonlight. He had an honest, open face, and it sounded like an adventure I shouldn't miss, so I agreed to stay overnight at his parents' house. These simple village people gave us some dinner, and after dark we left on his motorcycle. It was a slow ride across dirt roads, the olive trees silvery in the bright moonlight. The landscape had a ghostly air, and I tried to capture with my eyes everything I saw so as never to forget it. At the temple complex, the full moon was high in the sky, and we were alone. The young man, whose name I no longer remember, began to make romantic overtures, but I was quite firm with him and, luckily, he did not insist. In silence, we walked around the temple, precisely delineated but also mysterious in the moonlight, and then returned to his parents' house. I was shown to my small room with a wooden board and thin mattress and, although very tired, found it hard to sleep. The next day we exchanged addresses, and I boarded the first boat for Hydra.

I had a meal in a restaurant on the waterfront. There was nothing very special about the owner but he was lively, dark and very attentive. I felt intensely attracted to him and ended up in his bed, making violent love. The next day, I was no longer the slightest bit interested and wondered what I had seen in him. He, on the contrary, couldn't believe that a woman he had made love to would be able to reject him so completely, so soon. He appeared to go mad, following me around, begging, threatening. I couldn't understand his behaviour. Men often dropped women after a one-night stand, so why couldn't a woman do the same?

Someone at the Beat Hotel had suggested I visit a famous writer and poet who lived on Hydra, in a house at the very top of the village. There were no phones. I simply appeared at his house and told him that Gregory Corso had said I should visit him. He invited me to drink coffee on his terrace, where he told me the disturbing story of his wife's near-death car accident. She was a painter. Most of her bones had been broken, her right arm so badly he wondered whether she would ever use it again. He spoke coldly, perhaps to conceal his feelings. He told me he was proud of her courage and her willpower. She was learning to use her left hand to draw. He then read my fortune, looking expertly at the patterns left by my Turkish coffee grains, swirling what was left of the thick liquid in the small cup and then turning it upside down on a plate.

'Some people carry a sword, but you will carry a cross.'

I left his house disgruntled and depressed. I had felt so strong, independent and victorious, but a few words from the 'oracle' had cast me down, put me in my place.

As I walked down the hill, away from the village, I stumbled and hurt my foot on a stone. It bled and I thought of his courageous wife. Was that a story he had invented to disturb me? I felt I had met a man who hated women.

Throughout the 1960s, you could pick up mail and money at American Express offices. I remember using one in Venice, just near or on Piazza San Marco, and in Athens, on Syntagma Square. Caresse wrote to me c/o American Express, asking me to meet her in Delphi. On the way there, I passed through Thebes, birthplace of Oedipus, a name that conjured up visions of ancient Greece, and was disappointed by its humble appearance. Delphi was also a village, its former grandeur confined to the still-majestic ruins. Along its main street, shops were hung with brightly coloured wool carpets. In front of shops and private houses, black-clad older women spun yarn and gossiped, eyeing the passing foreigners. Caresse took me to see the plot of land where she hoped to build a Centre for World Peace. 'Delphi is the perfect place for my centre,' she told me excitedly. She had a meeting planned with the mayor. We walked up the Sacred Way to the temple of Apollo, wound through smaller treasuries and temples to the theatre and, highest of all, to the athletic stadium. This wild mountain region seemed the appropriate place for humans to salute divine cosmic forces, a perfect choice for her idealistic dream. I left Delphi before her meeting with the mayor, but Caresse wrote later to tell me that the Greeks had got cold feet and backed out of their offer of support.

I wanted to see more of Greece and especially what was left of its ancient civilization. Since I couldn't repair Takis's old studio, I was now free to travel. I decided that after meeting Caresse in Delphi, I would drive across the Peloponnese. I drove to Olympia, taking the ferry across the strait of Itea, inspired by the energy of the Delphic landscape. In Olympia, I admired the great reliefs, long fallen from the temple architraves and now displayed in a museum. So unlike Delphi, nestling among mountainous crags, Olympia, the ancient centre of the Olympic Games dedicated to Zeus, was surrounded by olive and chestnut trees in the rich agricultural land of the Peloponnese. I remember being quite alone in the museum and walking slowly through the ruins, trying to imagine what this great centre might have felt like more than a thousand years earlier. In Epidaurus, I met a Greek girl about my own age whose name I loved:

Eleftheria (Freedom). She was my proud guide to the amphitheatre, where one could hear a whisper from the highest stone rows. The ancient Greeks understood how sound travelled better than we do and built their outdoor theatres in a shell-like form.

On my way to Mycenae, I stopped in Tiryns and walked through the cyclopean tunnel of stones, worn smooth by the passage of centuries of sheep, flocks huddling there as a protection against winter winds or driving rain, their soft coats polishing the great stones as they pressed against them.

I arrived in Mycenae late in the afternoon and drove straight up to the tombs. I walked alone through the Lion Gate and into the tomb of Agamemnon and, a little way in, found myself in total darkness. I wasn't sure how far it went nor how large it was and, as I crept nervously forward, reaching out to feel for the walls, I felt the spirit of Agamemnon beside me. The presence was so strong that I turned and moved quickly towards the light and out. I climbed up to the acropolis in the twilight, imagining the grandeur of the Mycenaean palace overlooking the Argolide plain in all directions – south towards Tiryns and Argos, north towards Corinth. I sat looking over the valley, smoking a joint, and noticed shards of pottery, fragments of painted figures, scattered among the stones at my feet, and wondered why they had been discarded. I carefully stowed some in my car and drove to the small inn where amateur archaeologist Heinrich Schliemann had stayed when he discovered the tombs and so carelessly dug out their treasures. The walls of the inn proudly displayed photographs of him and his team. While I waited for my dinner to be served, I drew the figure that had haunted me in the dark tomb. The head was based entirely on ellipses, and I wrote a poem I conceived as the cosmogony of the human face.

In the light of the next day, the shards I had collected were ordinary bits of broken pottery, bearing no trace of the marks I had imagined in my hash-induced hallucinations in the evening dusk. In the daylight, I walked into Agamemnon's tomb again and saw how much smaller it was than I had imagined, although now I could see and appreciate the extraordinary height and structure of its beehive ceiling.

I returned through Tiryns and walked, once again alone, through the huge walls and marvelled at the thoughts of those who had built them, their reasons for using such enormous rocks and their skill in fitting them so perfectly together. The remains of the Titans.

It was the end of the summer, and time to keep my appointment with Takis in Venice. After two days at sea, my ferry glided into the city, shrouded in an autumnal mist, domes and spires reflecting the last rays of the hidden sun. I arrived exhausted and filthy, to be met by Takis and taken to the Danieli Hotel. In its luxurious velvet interior, I felt conspicuously out of place. All I wanted was sleep. And sleep I did, in sheets of silk, awaking to red roses and champagne, a room-service dinner and much love-making. Takis said he had missed me terribly. I believed him and felt comforted to be back in his protective embrace. In my youthful naivety, I fancied that he had made the long train voyage because he couldn't wait to see me, but the next day I felt disappointed when it became apparent that he had unconnected motivations. One was to have an inflatable rubber man made somewhere in Venice. Takis was preparing for his exhibition at the Iris Clert Gallery and, once he had welcomed me in style, his focus returned entirely to his work.

Having made the necessary purchases, we sped back to Paris in my TR3 to inflate the Michelin man that he had bought in Venice at the garage on the boulevard Raspail.

The First Man in Space

NOVEMBER 1960

Sinclair came repeatedly to our apartment. Takis had made him a blue 'spacesuit', and they both wore these one-piece jumpsuits that zipped up the front. I walked down boulevard Saint-Germain sandwiched between two tall, spacesuit-clad men, to stop at the Old Navy for coffee and Gauloises. Takis thought he was creating a new fashion that everyone would soon wear.

To open his exhibition at the Iris Clert Gallery, *L'Impossible: Un Homme dans l'Espace*, Takis decided to launch a poet into space. Sinclair was to be strapped into a rudimentary steel seat and, once hoisted up near the wall-fixed electromagnet, he would hover two metres above the floor. From this precarious position, Sinclair planned to read a poem dedicated to the dismantling of all atomic weapons.

Although Takis promised to make him the first man in space, Sinclair was not satisfied. His daily visits, prior to the vernissage, were mainly to urge Takis to buy him a helmet. He was concerned that the magnetic field would damage his brain. Takis cruelly kept him in suspense. Just before the night of the opening the helmet was purchased. On the evening of the vernissage, the smallest gallery in Paris was packed. Also floating, attracted to a huge horned magnet, was the inflated Michelin man Takis had bought in Venice.

On the evening of the opening on 29 November 1960, there was an intense air of excitement, of nervous anticipation fuelled by soft drugs and wine. Sinclair fulfilled every expectation: bent double in a foetal position, encased in spacesuit and glass-fibre helmet, voice tremulous and words deeply felt, he read out his declaration of a Poet in Space:

> I am a sculpture. There are other sculptures like me. The main difference is that they cannot speak. When some of the sculptures try to speak, they explode. They cause death . . . I would like to see all

the nuclear bombs on Earth turned into sculptures . . .*

In April 1961, Gagarin was launched in *Sputnik* as the first man in space and his name was spread across the front page of the *International Herald Tribune*. Sinclair, whose poetic purity and belief in metaphor had convinced him that he was first to float in space, rang the editor to protest their headline. All Paris had seen him, hadn't they been informed?

Corso commented that it was Sinclair's fault. He should have made sure the event had more publicity before the show opened. Had he rung the newspapers and urged them to send reporters to witness his performance at the vernissage? No, of course he hadn't, because Sinclair thought that the world should have been watching as he was lifted into space.

It was during this period that Sinclair wrote the

* An excerpt from Sinclair Beiles's poem 'I am a Sculpture' read 'in space' during the opening of *L'Impossible*, an exhibition of Takis's works: *L'Impossible: Un Homme dans l'Espace*, Galerie Iris Clert, Paris 1960.

wonderful long poem that I still consider one of his greatest, with the title I remember as 'Homage to the Pioneers of Space'. Starting with the Wright brothers, Sinclair eulogized every engineer and scientist who had made space flight possible, including Gagarin. He read it to us and then handed Takis the many pages of typescript for safe-keeping.

Some months later, Sinclair asked me to show him my poems. He read them and then asked why I didn't have them published: 'They are as good as anyone else's.' Then he took out a sheet of paper and offered it to me. It was a typewritten stanza from his 'Pioneers of Space' poem, with his signature at the bottom, in his round, carefully formed handwriting. I still have my page, but where is the entire 'Homage to the Pioneers of Space'? Has it survived? Did Takis keep it safe? I never saw it again.*

* I embedded the stanza Sinclair gave me in *Faster Than Birds Poemdrum*. Knowing that Sinclair suffered from a mental disorder that, at times, shattered his crystal-clear vision into painful splinters, in 2009 I fragmented the short stanza of text by laser-cutting the words on to three drums, each nested inside the other. Each drum rotates at a different speed and in the opposite direction to the others. Words and letters,

Everything after the *L'Impossible* exhibition seemed anticlimactic. Yves Klein had heard about it and, in an act of jealous rivalry, staged his 'leap into the void', photographs which show him throwing himself into the air from a first-floor window. The performance was carefully staged and Klein dramatically swan-dived from a first-floor window into a net or tarpaulin held by his Judo students. Klein then had the photographs doctored and dated the event two days prior to the *Impossible* opening. He circulated his own newspaper with the headline: 'A man in space! The painter of space leaps into the void!' Pierre Restany, Klein's extremely vocal polemicist, defended him, and Takis enlisted Alain Jouffroy to support his original work with magnetism in a defiant newspaper article. Takis was sleepless, intensely aware that his work was about to be purloined by Klein, perhaps the only person to see its true worth and importance. Klein claimed to be able to make objects float without the use of strings! Takis thought that Klein would use an

---

illuminated from within, are dislocated in an intermingling of meaning and light. I feel certain that Sinclair would have approved.

electromagnet, or even high-pressured air, to float an object. Takis had attached objects with string on purpose, to make the pull of the magnetic force visible. It was his poetic way of illustrating magnetic attraction. Takis was in constant contact with Iris, who was also Klein's gallerist and in constant contact with him. To end it, Yves made the mistake of sending Iris an express letter from Cascia in Umbria, where he was visiting the convent of Santa Rita. He predated the letter, declaring that the use of magnetism was his invention, and said he had sent a letter to himself as a form of copyright. Iris finally realized that Takis's fears were real and broke off with Klein, refusing to show him again.

New York and the Curious Episode of Salvador Dalí's Moustache

DECEMBER 1960

Living with Takis was difficult and his extreme anxiety, following Yves Klein's well-publicized 'leap into the void', was also taking its toll on me. I was unsure of my next step in my own work, the surge of development of the year before having slowed to a near stop. I needed to be alone, and my Christmas visit to Geneva to see my father only strengthened my feeling that I had to put some distance between myself and both men. Takis agreed it would be good if I returned to New York, taking two of his sculptures to deliver to Martha Jackson. Thus began a restless period, during which I lived both in Paris and New York, unable to decide where I belonged. Perhaps because of my relationship with my father, whose personality could have crushed my own, whom I loved and hated, to whom I looked for approval and encouragement, who I knew was counting on me to fulfil the void he felt, I seemed always to be looking for men who would endorse me. I found them easily, then discovered their need to control, unmasking their own insecurity. Takis, who was fifteen years older, did nurture me but he also found my progress as a young artist threatening. I needed to live on my own for a while and I did exactly that.

I crossed the Atlantic once more by boat, with numerous trunks and my racing-green TR3, since I intended to stay for a long time. I must have stayed in a hotel, possibly the Stanhope, or perhaps my mother and her husband, André, were staying there, because its telephone number is scribbled on a note book page filled with sketches of magnets.

Takis and I had met an American composer living on the Giudecca who had given me his New York address. I visited him just after arriving in the city. He was busy restoring a small town house. I told him that I had all my suitcases and my car in customs, and I wasn't sure how to get them out. He introduced me then and there to a young

Italian who was helping him deal with city officials and builders, assuring me that he knew
everyone and would be able to retrieve my car
and belongings without too much trouble. Gianni
was short and stocky with a toothy smile, greased-
back black hair and a smart suit. He drove me to
the airport the next day to get all my things
released. Whenever we passed a policeman directing traffic, Gianni would stop and have a friendly
chat. I soon had car and suitcases, but I needed a
place to live. Gianni told me he knew a very nice
place uptown on the West Side, where rooms were
reasonable. It was a respectable, safe, girls' pension, no guests allowed after hours. I didn't like
the sound of it and began to feel that smiling
Gianni was possibly a member of a family I wanted
to stay well away from. He had other ideas. He
wanted to date me, and I found it very difficult to
escape his persistent attentions. He began ringing
me at all hours, even waking me at four in the
morning, but I kept my cool and finally managed
to convince him that I was not interested.

Martha Jackson had met Takis the summer
before at the Venice Biennale and had asked him to
send her two magnetic sculptures for a client she

thought would like them. Takis took them apart to make them easier to pack and made sketches, which I still have, showing me how to put them together and how to install them.

Martha Jackson invited me to the opening of her next exhibition, by the Catalan artist Antoni Tàpies. I had unwisely invited Amy Mims to meet me there. Alan Ansen had declared her a great genius in Venice the summer before and I had been jealous of her then. She wasn't very pretty, but she was clever and had graduated from Harvard, whereas I hadn't even attended university – unless my short time at the Sorbonne counted. She was supposedly writing a great book that would be the equivalent of James Joyce's *Ulysses*. Instead, she met Takis's best friend, the cartoonist Minos Argyrakis, who suffered from manic depression, and would go to live with him in Athens.

At the gallery, Amy was waiting for me in a big purple hat, with a broad smile. The large matter-imbued paintings were half obscured by animated clusters of people. A young man came over, and I realized it was Joan Artigas* from the École du

* Joan Gardy Artigas is a Catalan ceramicist, artist and was a close collaborator with Joan Miró.

Louvre. Only about eighteen months earlier we had agreed that the classes were mind-numbingly dull. We had met again in Paris but had drifted apart during my intense relationship with Jean-Jacques. It seemed as if years separated those two moments in a time elastic and swollen with events. Joan saw me, said, 'Oh, Liliane, it's great to see you again,' and was gone. A few minutes later, I heard someone scream, but there were so many people I didn't notice where it came from. Joan reappeared with an immaculate white napkin in his hand and, with an exaggerated bow, presented it to me, as with a great treasure, saying, 'Une homage à la belle Liliane.'

I carefully unfolded it and there was a puzzling object: black, oily, pointed to a fine tip and looking very much like a rat's tail.

'What is it?'

'It's Dalí's moustache. I cut it off in your honour.'

Dalí, at the far side of the room, was shouting, 'Press, press, where are the photographers? This is a scandal! A scoundrel has cut off my moustache.'

Dalí knew damn well who had cut it off, because Joan was the son of the great Spanish ceramicist who made all Dalí's ceramic objects and had also collaborated with Picasso and Miró.* Joan had known Dalí from childhood.

This event threw Amy into a jealous fit. She couldn't understand why she hadn't been the recipient of such homage when there she stood, brilliant and beautiful in her unique purple hat. She had already downed several glasses of champagne, because, she said, she was Irish and apart from being the world's greatest poets they were also the heaviest drinkers. To endure the neglect, she drank even more, and at the end of the evening stood sentinel at the door, blessing everyone who went into the night. Being so totally off her head, she was unable to tell me where she lived, and I took her back to my loft. She casually disrobed and collapsed, while Dalí's moustache mysteriously vanished.

After that evening, Amy and Minos often visited. They'd married in a ceremony in Central Park. Amy showed me her lace veil and said a poet friend had acted as priest. Poets were the true celebrants,

* Josep Llorens i Artigas (16 June 1892 –11 December 1980) was a Spanish ceramic artist known for his collaboration with Joan Miró. He is credited with relaunching ceramics as a European art form.

after all. I still see her with field flowers in her hair, eyes filled with heavenly fantasies. Or perhaps not so heavenly since she wanted to join the IRA to fight the English. When I showed them my latest experimental works with plastic, Minos said he preferred my earlier gouache *Sky Scrolls*. No matter what I was doing, people always seemed to prefer what I had done in the past.

I met Iris Clert by chance at a gallery opening and she introduced me to Chryssa, a stocky Greek artist, who worked with neon. Iris couldn't find enough words to express her admiration for Chryssa's work and she also told me that Chryssa wanted to rent out her loft on Broadway and 18th Street for three months. I was desperate to move out of my run-down hotel and happily agreed to rent it.

Chryssa's loft took up the width of a whole New York city block. The main space was reached up a flight of narrow, dimly lit stairs to a small hallway. Two further floors were reached from inside the first huge space. Grimy, barely translucent, floor-to-ceiling windows faced Broadway, allowing some light to enter the front of the space, while the rest folded into shadows, the kitchen at the back dark, except for one bare light bulb. Stairs at the back led to another space that was smaller and much more luminous, which I used as my studio. At the back there were stairs again and windows leading to a dark roof terrace with a fire escape. This was a frightening place, where bums came to sleep late at night, their noises keeping me awake. One night, I called my cousin Harold, who had lived in lofts, and he assured me that they wouldn't bother me, but asked if I wanted him to come over. I was brave enough to go it alone, placing a large kitchen knife beside my bed. The filth was commensurate with the size of the loft, and I didn't have the courage or strength to attempt to clean the huge floor. Harold advised me to hire a sailor, since they were used to swabbing decks, which I did. After that first 'spring clean', I never thought of cleaning it again. It was the perfect studio, a place where I could experiment with materials without worrying about cleaning or clearing. A couple of months later, when I went to visit Paul Cummings in his uptown apartment, I felt distinctly claustrophobic.

Paul came from a well-to-do Catholic family in Minnesota and, although he knew, or knew about, everyone in the New York art world, he was never completely accepted. As a student, he had lived in London, in Camden Square, studying set design at RADA. From the theatre, his interests had shifted to poetry and art. He had a large and important collection of first-edition contemporary poetry. Paul often came to look at my work, we'd go to exhibitions, and he'd take me to dinner. Our relationship was always one of friendship, although, at first, I felt that he had a crush on me.

With the help of a backer, Paul became co-director of the Louis Alexander Gallery and asked me to exhibit in an early group show several of the *Sky Scrolls* I'd brought with me. Few art dealers were interested in showing drawings, since they were difficult to sell. Paul felt that it was essential to look at artists' drawings to comprehend their more complex works. He was the first person to speak seriously to me about the importance of drawings.

Encouraged by his interest, I asked if he would give me a solo show, but he explained that I was still too young, that I might easily decide to abandon art, have babies or move into another profession. Some years later, Clement Greenberg told me to come back to him after I turned forty, at which age he could take me seriously as an artist. As a woman, I realized, I would always be too young.

Over the many years of our friendship, I would meet Paul mainly in New York, and walk the galleries, from uptown in the 70s through 57th Street, and later down to SoHo. Paul was my closest male friend. He was my height and, even when I first met him, stocky and wide-chested. His hands and his head were very large, somehow out of proportion to his body. His hands were also very fleshy, and sometimes, on meeting, in a particularly effusive mood, he would take both my hands in his. That was as close as he got, and I often wondered whether he had amorous relations with anyone. He lived alone in a one-bedroom apartment, his living-room walls covered in books and a few very select drawings. Paul was an excellent cook and made a point of knowing all the best restaurants in Manhattan. I remember being impressed by the editions of poetry that he had published, not to speak of his almost encyclopaedic knowledge.*

* Although I felt that Paul never quite forgave me for leaving New York, we would remain friends until his early death at the age of sixty-four in 1997.

Working with Light

Searching for a transparent world, I have come across a plastic, Plexiglass. Experimenting, I succeeded in getting very fine lines. I became conscious of how this accident happened and repeated it, making a 'painting' composed almost solely of these fine lines. Because of these fine lines, the transparent quality of the plastic was being used. But still, looking at the 'painting' I could see through it, see whatever was behind it and had nothing to do with the world of the 'painting'.

I wanted an interior transparency within the painting itself. Putting the 'painting' against the wall, I observed that the lines cast shadows thus duplicating themselves. This may be considered a simple visual effect, but for me, it was a very significant discovery. <u>It was the discovery of inner transparency, of the 'painting' and its double</u>. (Winter 1961)

The year before, when I had first visited Canal Street, I had started buying different types of plastic in small pieces in a store called Industrial Plastics Supply. I wanted to see how they behaved when I burned them. I set them on fire and watched as they melted or shrunk and carbonized. I had wanted to work with fire even before my discovery of Tefonstift, when I found that by vibrating the plastic stick, the molten material extruded in fine threads that I could draw with in the air, allowing them to settle on a clear sheet of Plexiglass.

I used a small hand-held torch to permanently fuse the plastic threads with the Plexiglass. The finished works were at times explosive but could also be gentle and labyrinthine, threads crossing and criss-crossing. I was immersed in Robert Graves's *Greek Myths* and the complex webs of my new works reminded me of Ariadne's threads that would guide Theseus out of the Minotaur's labyrinth. Mine was the path out of my murky unconscious into, I hoped, the luminous world of consciousness.

I was completely absorbed by my new works and felt a great freedom working alone in my upstairs studio. But, despite the elation of the new works, my diaries speak of my loneliness.

The city's art scene was bubbling with excitement, and I was invited, or went uninvited, with my friend Juliet, whom I saw frequently, to numerous openings, often of pop art, the works almost always made by men. Juliet wrote and painted, but her stepfather insisted that she take a job. I never really knew where she worked but was impressed by her independence. One of the few women artists shown at the Castelli Gallery was Lee Bontecou, whose patchwork metal relief sculptures with dark voids at their centre I found oddly disturbing. They looked like the sewn-together skins of tortured beings, the central hole suggesting vaginal screams. Leo Castelli was quite approachable and at one of his openings I spoke to him of my new works, and he asked me to bring a few into the gallery. I brought in some smaller Plexiglass and Tefon-stift works, which I called *Fire Lines*. Leo and his assistant Ivan Karp looked at them. Ivan said they reminded him of Pollock's paintings. I countered that the resemblance was only superficial. Leo simply smiled. Ivan told me I should look at Lee Bontecou's work and said he would introduce me to her.

On the day I was to meet Ivan and Lee for dinner, all my wisdom teeth had been pulled out by my dentist, Mr Richman.* Heavily sedated with painkillers and hardly able to speak, I felt like dropping out, but my curiosity prevailed. Lee was reserved and spoke very little. She looked very young and boyish. Luckily, Ivan had decided that we would go to a movie and then to a Szechuan restaurant in Brooklyn. By the time we left the cinema, my medication had worn off and I was in real pain. Ivan recommended hot and sour soup for the pain – my first taste of highly spiced food. I got through the evening but couldn't wait to get back to my loft.

At openings, I would be invited to parties or to join artists at the Cedar Bar on Houston Street. There I was introduced to Franz Kline, who invited me to his studio, but instead I took an interested collector to see my new works with fire. Another artist I met at the Castelli Gallery was Victoria Barr. I met

* Mr Richman was one of the discoverers of nitrous oxide, known as laughing gas.

her at a private view of Frank Stella's paintings – I saw her from behind, noticing her very long hair, when she suddenly turned and introduced herself. We next met a year or so later, when Iranian artist Bahman Farman-Farmaian, whom we knew as Farman and who had studied art at Yale at the same time as Victoria, generously took us out to dinner: Takis and I, Victoria, plus the novelists Iris Owens and William Burroughs. Victoria, whose father, Alfred Barr, had founded MoMA, was, to the chagrin of both her parents, a painter. I think of her as a colourist, her palette intense and romantic. Her thoughtful and circumspect behaviour concealed a deep emotional well that surfaced in her paintings. Iris and Victoria had both had love relationships with Farman, although Iris's continued through much of the rest of her life. Farman was heir to a large fortune but his political activities in New York supported the extreme left. Ironically, Iris wanted Farman to buy her a mink coat – after all, she had married him to give him an American passport. Years later, he would buy her that coat before returning to Iran, hoping to join the revolution.

In his frequent letters, in a misspelled,

awkwardly printed hand, Takis wrote of his love and how much he missed me. With the coming of spring, he suggested I return to Paris, at least for a short visit. I was happy to do so, but not so thrilled to be greeted by a dishevelled woman when I knocked on the door of his room at the Hôtel La Louisiane. Seeing me, she shut the door, which was subsequently opened by Takis himself, apologetically telling me to leave my bags and go for a coffee at a nearby café.

Takis was all charm and sweetness. He missed me so much and was so excited by my imminent arrival that he just could not spend the night alone. I was his pure and adorable child, his great love. Of course, sometimes he fucked other women, but weren't we free spirits? I was hurt, as if internally bruised, and knew that our relationship had entered a disturbingly different phase.

Another Interruption

My father announced that he was going to Israel for Easter and invited Takis and me to go with him. He didn't tell me that he was also taking his latest girlfriend and her eight-year-old son. Antoinette was from an aristocratic Hungarian family and had been married to a famous Hungarian photographer. Her background somewhat intimidated my father, and his generous invitation was prompted by his need for our support. Suddenly, the fact that Takis was a well-known artist had a value. It was my first visit to Israel, and we were both curious to see the country. I knew that many of my relatives lived there, where my father had managed to send them to escape the Holocaust. During my childhood, my mother and grandmother had sent frequent packages of clothes and canned food to my uncle in Tel Aviv. My father wanted to visit every one of his and my mother's relations and he particularly wanted me to meet them.

Two visits are still fresh in my memory. The first was to the home of my father's cousin Yitta, the mother of my cousin Yehuda Skurnick. I didn't meet Yehuda, because he was in the air force, and I don't remember meeting my favourite cousin, Gabi, who was studying at MIT, but I did meet his brother Toli, after whom my parents had named their first child, who had died of pneumonia just a year before I was born. Toli had an exceptional memory and told me stories about our fathers' histories that I had not heard before. Perhaps because of this talent, Toli became a politician, like his father, Hermann Segall, after whom a street is named in Tel Aviv.

My most vivid memory is of our visit to my mother's brother, Mietek, and his family in their small apartment in Ramat Gan. I was curious to meet my three younger cousins, Iris, Beni and Mira. Mietek, who had been so talented as a boy, drove a taxi for a living. His beautiful wife, Ester, was a nurse and the main breadwinner. She was strong, lively and dynamic, very similar in character to my grandmother, Mietek's mother. Mietek was slow and clearly a pessimist. The two girls were shy, but Beni was talkative. I felt oppressed in the hot, stuffy apartment, where, even standing, we filled the small living room. I wanted desperately to escape. Takis thought it might be fun to explore the area. My uncle was very much against our leaving, saying they had food prepared and that nothing would be open, since it was both Easter and Shabbat. I knew that leaving would be insensitive, but my father, his girlfriend and her son would stay, and I wanted to get away from my depressing uncle.

The streets were empty, apart from a few old Arab men sitting on doorsteps. We found an Arab café open, where we ate very well, although not the kind of food that Mietek would have approved of. This little exploratory walk gave us the idea to hire a jeep and drive to Jerusalem.

Mietek was very much against our plan, saying the road was bad and we would run out of petrol before reaching a station. Beni was enthusiastic and I could see that he wanted to join us. He was so bright and full of life, no one could have predicted that he would be struck by schizophrenia at nineteen – when Israelis do their army service. His experience of army life triggered his illness, but I always felt that his father played some part.

Takis and I drove off and, as predicted, were out of petrol in less than an hour from Tel Aviv, stuck on the empty road, when who should turn up but Mietek with Beni waving to us halfway out of the car window. Having helped us out, they drove back to Tel Aviv while we continued, driving on dirt roads, swallowed by dust in our open jeep. I did all the driving, extremely proud that I could drive this by no means easy vehicle. Takis was my navigator, trying to decipher the Hebrew map we'd bought, confidently instructing me to take the wrong road, ending up in olive groves and dead-end villages. I remember the approach to the ancient city, driving uphill on a road lined with countless saplings, planted, I found out later, by young Israelis with donations from Jews abroad. When we finally arrived in Jerusalem, I suggested we go to the King David Hotel. Leaving our jeep to the attendants, we walked into the elegant foyer like two bums, sunburned, exhausted and covered in dust. Takis distributed tips and, to our surprise, they found us a room. I guess there weren't that many tourists in Jerusalem in April 1961.

And then the trip was over. It had been an emotional journey, another interruption, disturbing the creative flow of my work. Although I had been excited and happy to see Takis after three months on my own, and we had both enjoyed the trip to Israel, my feelings on meeting for the first time these close members of my family were disturbing, and it was a relief to interrupt the familial visits to explore the country. I felt troubled by their emotional greetings that placed me back into the seething world of my childhood.

I was suddenly home in my New York loft, alone, everything exactly as I had left it. It seemed as if I had never left New York, as if the travels, sights, sounds, smells, Takis, my father and his girl-friend, and my Israeli relatives were all part of a long and complex dream.

I was happy to be in New York, working again, but it wasn't easy to get back into the same rhythm that I'd had before the trip. I continued working on *Fire Lines* and noticed that extreme heat directed to one spot would melt away the threads, so that they appeared burst or exploded into tiny segments moving outwards, away from the point of heat.

I still loved living in the spacious loft, the dirt and mess allowing me a degree of freedom I would never have had in a more ordered environment. But I started having blinding headaches and feelings of nausea. I couldn't hold down any food and became so alarmed that I called a doctor, who decided that I had to go into hospital for tests to make sure I didn't have a serious brain disease. In the Bellevue hospital ward, I complained about the fluorescent lighting, kept on day and night, the terrible food and crowded wards, and did yoga exercises in between being wheeled out for brain scans. Eventually, they let me out, having found nothing seriously wrong. I decided that my headaches and nausea were the result of my inhaling the Tefon-stift fumes. I wondered how much Teflon the sticks contained, and whether it was toxic, and decided to switch to a clear acrylic monomer.

When my mother found out I was in hospital, alarm bells rang across the Atlantic between my parents. Now living in Florida with André, she rushed to New York. My father cabled her the wherewithal to rent a small apartment in Manhattan, on 12th Street and 6th Avenue, and I bid a sad farewell to my loft and joined her. She decided that

I was run-down and needed looking after. My works were stored for the two or three weeks we spent together, my mother cooked all my favourite dishes and I spent most of my time reading. I remember the sunshine and the calm, but also the feeling of loss caused by the interruption in my creative flow.

Interruption had become a way of life. I never seemed to have sustained periods of stability to fully explore my early works with fire and plastics, although, despite the interruption over Easter, in the last six months I had lived in New York, I felt I had made great progress in my work. I complained of loneliness in my diaries and letters, but living alone was extremely fruitful and gave me a sense of my own strength and independence that I did not experience when I lived with Takis, who often treated me more like his child than as an equal partner.

I hadn't seen Merriman since leaving Solebury in the summer of 1955. Merriman had been a day student. Her parents lived just across the river in Lambertville, New Jersey, and were both artists. Her mother, Elsie Driggs, had been a well-known Precisionist painter before meeting her father, Lee

Gatch, who, an abstract expressionist, became the more famous of the two.

I met Merriman again through her father, whom by chance I met at an opening.

My parents were worried about my health and wanted me to rent a clean apartment and not another loft. I decided, with financial help from my father, to rent an unfurnished apartment. It was in a new building with underground parking on King Street, right in the heart of mafia Little Italy. Everyone said it was the safest place in New York. I could even garage my TR3 under the building. Merriman told me that she was also looking for a place to live and we decided to move into the new apartment together.

Merriman, who had come to school looking unlike any of the other girls, became an actress. I saw her on stage only once, when she invited me to a performance of John Millington Synge's *The Playboy of the Western World*. I was amazed at her transformation. She seemed to come alive on stage with a warmth and energy that was totally unlike her offstage persona.

The apartment was too small for me to work in and I needed to find a separate studio. I had continued to frequent Canal Street and had become friendly with Max Landau, the owner of the shop where I bought my sheets of Perspex. He owned the whole building, which was full of all kinds of plastics, from sheets of Perspex to cartons of moulded plastic baubles. I'd shown him one or two of the *Fire Lines* works, which he liked. He offered to clear a corner of the second floor for me to work in and told me to help myself to materials and machinery, which consisted of a large pillar drill and a table saw.

I began to drill into small blocks of Perspex, realizing that the empty holes I created appeared as solid when seen from the other side of the block. With his help and encouragement, I also used the table saw to cut parallel slices into thick Perspex sheets, then painting the back side white, the empty cuts appearing solid. I was excited about these new works and the endless possibilities that working there gave me.

A New Name

SUMMER 1961

At the end of June, I flew to Paris to meet Takis. The first three days were heaven. We were so happy together; we hardly saw anyone else. On the fourth day, reality set in. Takis had taken a room in a cheap hotel. In the confined space, we began to get on each other's nerves. First thing in the morning, Takis would go down to the Old Navy for coffee and cigarettes with Raymondos and other Greek friends. After all the healthy food my mother had prepared, I wanted to start the day eating fruit from the market that lined the rue de Seine. I realized how different our rhythms had grown. Then, suddenly, I had a sore throat, headache and such a high fever that I was in a delirium. It was summer and Takis couldn't find a doctor. Finally, a friend sent us to an old doctor they knew. We had to go to him, since he had something wrong with his legs.

I remember floating slowly down the stairs, Takis practically carrying me up them on our return. The old doctor looked me over and said I had a serious infection caused by my tonsils, that I had to have them taken out since they were permanently inflamed and would cause kidney problems and eventually a rheumatic heart. I rang my father and he sent me a ticket to fly to Geneva, where the doctor first thought I had scarlet fever. It turned out to be a very severe strep throat that was quickly overcome with the help of antibiotics. While convalescing in my father's apartment, I meditated on the shifting moiré patterns of the fine mesh curtains as they slowly stirred veil-like in the breeze.

As soon as I was well enough, Takis and I went to Venice just in time for the Biennale and decided to stay the whole summer on the Giudecca at the Casa Frollo, a charming villa with a large garden, where we had a room overlooking the waterway at a discounted artist price. The Biennale was entirely contained in the Giardini, with national pavilions showing that year's favoured artist or group. We went to the preview and were invited to any number of parties. Iris Clert and Iolas were selling Takis's works and their collectors wanted to meet him.

I had brought one or two of my *Fire Lines* and was asked to exhibit in an alternative Biennale, the Premio Biennale di Georgione, in the Museo di Castelfranco, a small town near Venice. Our friends discussed the short biography I had to put together for the catalogue. John, the American composer who had helped me on my arrival in New York, and who lived with his family near the Casa Frollo, suggested I change my name. Liliane Segall was not musical enough and was already taken by the pop artist George Segal. I didn't want to be associated with Segal's white plaster men in so intimate a manner as one's family name. I also had a distant cousin, Lazar Segall, a famous painter in Brazil, and on the rare occasions I signed my work I'd used *L. Segall*. What potential for confusion! I had already thought of changing my name in the autumn of '58 and had reversed my names, signing myself Nahil Lages. I should have stuck to that. It had an original ring to it. But John convinced me to keep my first name and change Segall to Line. In Italian – in which I was fluent, and we were in Venice – it is pronounced 'Leené'. So, in the small catalogue of this exhibition I was Liliane Line.

Names are difficult. I have never got used to

mine. It did not seem to fit me, or I didn't fit into it, like a suit that is too large or too small. After twenty years with Liliane Segall, I hadn't identified with her. Perhaps a bit with Liliane, but the two names together didn't seem right. I would have preferred my mother's maiden name, Kustanowicz (although my grandmother had resigned herself to Kast when the immigration officials complained that her Russian name was too long for an American citizen).

Back in New York, I realized that Line was line, and all my work was threads and lines. It wouldn't do. I took away the 'e', but Lin looked too Chinese (I had not yet met the painter Richard Lin). I inserted a 'j' between the 'i' and the 'n' for a more interesting look, but pronounced it 'Lin'. I was satisfied but hadn't realized that the name change would hide me from those who already knew me. I had given myself yet another veil. I was fascinated by veils.

During our stay in Venice, we saw Manina often, happily living with Domingo and his boyfriend, two very sweet men. Although she had exhibitions of her paintings in Venice, they were not included in major surrealist shows. It wasn't enough to meet people once every two years at the Biennale, an artist had to live in cities that were magnetic centres for art. After Nina's murder, Manina had written letters supposedly from Nina to read to her mother. Possibly through this painful but comforting habit, Nina's spirit had come to inhabit Manina. When she finally returned to her art, her paintings were very similar to Nina's vibrant colours and broad brush strokes, and very different from her former delicate and finely detailed work. In later years, Manina turned to three-dimensional objects, talismans and jewellery.

Manina taught me to throw yarrow sticks or coins to question the I Ching. From my first sight of her in Grand Central Station, I had decided that she was a good witch, a Faery Queen. It seemed natural that she would produce objects that could offer protection and, therefore, so much the worse that she could not have protected her only child. Our relationship was uneasy, although she did write me a long and tender letter after I told her that I wanted to write about Nina and our friendship. In time, she met Sky, a lovely young American, who helped fill the emotional void Nina's death had caused.

Takis and I met Hundertwasser, the Austrian painter who had helped me find my first Parisian apartment. He had bought a palazzo on the

Giudecca near the Casa Frollo, where he lived with his demure, kimono-clad Japanese wife. His constant insistence on his work had worked. He was now famous and apparently wealthy. He offered to show us his studio on the large *piano nobile* of the palazzo. I marvelled at the luxury compared to our modest nomadic life. Takis said Hundertwasser had sold out with naively decorative paintings. I thought it might have had more to do with his behaviour; he was his own dealer and knew where his every painting was. He also never forgot a name!

We regularly met up with Alan Ansen, who often had other poets staying with him, Gregory Corso or Allen Ginsberg. He would hold forth on his latest work or local gossip as he prepared his dizzying Martinis. He announced that Peggy Guggenheim was throwing a big party on her birthday, and he was writing a short play in her honour, to be performed on the evening. It was about three astronauts on a mission to the moon, one of whom was a woman. Alan asked me to play the female part. Takis offered to make papier-mâché masks. I became the first woman to walk on the moon, in the fragrant penumbra of Peggy's garden, the shadows of her many guests still before me. Afterwards, people enquired whether I was an actress — it seems that I was the only one to speak my lines clearly.

Takis did not swim so, despite it being very hot and humid, we rarely went to the Lido to cool off. We spent our days making love, sitting in cafés with friends or taking in horror films or Laurel and Hardy in Italian. I was restless and thought of rowing to the quiet waters of the laguna to swim. Takis agreed to come and, with John's two sons, we rented a large rowboat from an upstream dock. Rowing downstream to the laguna was easy. Takis complimented himself on his rowing ability when the current was so strong that we would have easily drifted there without touching an oar. Once there, I jumped into the water, only to find it too shallow, with a slimy bottom. The children splashed about, but we soon tired and decided to return. Takis rowed back to the Zitelle, where he got off, feeling he had already done more than his share of rowing. The younger child left with him, but the older boy, who couldn't have been more than ten, stayed on valiantly to help me row the boat upstream and across the Giudecca. We slowly progressed upstream. In the middle of the water-way, I realized that we were less than halfway there and in danger of being overturned by the waves made by the huge ships that used the Giudecca. My young companion offered to row but hadn't the strength to overcome the downstream current. After struggling for more than two hours, I managed to cross the waterway and moor the boat, still a long way from where I'd rented it, but I couldn't row any more. I was badly sunburned and suffering from heatstroke. Our friend's son was certainly happy to get back home. On seeing me arrive crimson-faced and exhausted, Takis told me that it was a good experience; to push myself to complete exhaustion was healthy. He didn't appear to feel the slightest concern or guilt that he'd left me with a child to row up the Giudecca.

Neither of us was aware that I was in the first month of a pregnancy. When I started feeling sick, it was usually after meals. Takis would say that he felt sick too and complain that Venetian cooking was far too oily. The only foods I could eat were fruit, mozzarella and raw eggs.

The long summer slowly came to an end. Takis took the train back to Paris and I went to Milan, encumbered by an enormous suitcase, paintings and the exhibited *Fire Lines*. In Venice, Lucio Del Pezzo had given me his phone number and invited me to visit. On arrival in Milan, I phoned him and, after a moment of confusion, having forgotten who I was, he kindly invited me to visit his studio and have dinner in his home.

The next morning, having slept very little, I took the train to Geneva, arriving in the evening, completely exhausted and looking forward to a hot shower and comfortable bed. My father had other ideas. He needed me to accompany him to a dinner in Lausanne: 'Just take a shower and you'll feel fine. I need your presence. She is bringing her ex-husband, who is a famous photographer.'

Of course, I had the shower and went along to support him. 'She' was the Hungarian girlfriend who had come with us to Israel. She wanted to see how my father would stand up to her ex-husband, Ernst Haas. They also brought along a psychoanalyst friend. I sat between Ernst Haas and the psychoanalyst, my father's daughter, the artist on a visit from New York. The analyst quizzed me, as if my identity might be a fiction made up by my father to compete with Ernst Hass, whose photographs had been featured in MoMA's 1955 show, *The*

Family of Man. I remembered seeing the exhibition and his photograph of a small naked female child, sprawled face down in the luscious green vegetation of a forest glade. It may have been on the cover of the exhibition catalogue. A beautiful image: innocence and vulnerability slumbering in a natural paradise. I'd been struck by it, but my feelings were ambivalent. Was this innocence or had the child been raped and murdered? The small, white body, unmarked by age or experience, signified the extreme vulnerability and availability of the female sex. Its complete acceptance by the highest arbiters of the cultural canon was, at the very least, disturbing. We were all brainwashed by the reassuring concept of innocence, without wondering how often and how easily it was exploited and defiled.

During dinner, Haas was arrogant, patronizing me with ridiculous questions. I didn't get the chance to ask him about the naked girl child. In a move to impress them, I said I lived in an apartment just below West Village on King Street with an old schoolfriend, who was an actress. His next question was her name, and my mind went blank. Perhaps he thought I was lying, but this wasn't the first time my memory failed when put on the spot. I remembered people, but not their names. 'She' was Merriman Gatch.

Once, while I was working in his warehouse, Max Landau asked me out to dinner. Dorothy Miller was at the next table with a small group of people. She was an important curator at MoMA, whom I had met and who made weekly visits to artists' studios. I went to say hello. She remembered my name and introduced me to everyone, at which point I thought I needed to introduce Max, but forgot both his name and all of theirs, and stood awkwardly, poised as if in deep thought, then mumbled something and returned to my table.

It took me years to overcome this incapacity to remember people's names unless I had an ongoing relationship with them. I've asked myself many questions about this disability, the main one being, was I not really interested in other people, apart from those who became an integral part of my life? I didn't want to believe that, but I was also very sceptical, in general, about the 'art world'. Takis's paranoia and possessive behaviour only encouraged that alienation.

*

Back in Paris, I began to bleed. At first, I thought my period had returned, but the bleeding didn't stop. Iris Clert recommended her gynaecologist, who believed in natural medicine. He diagnosed an ectopic pregnancy and prescribed injections into my abdomen. Soon after, Takis and I took the SS *France* to New York. I was sick during the entire crossing and spent the days between the cinema and my bed, undergoing excruciating injections. In New York, my mother's gynaecologist, with a deft feel of my abdomen, proclaimed me three months pregnant with a healthy baby. When I asked about the bleeding, he told me not to worry, it would stop. On leaving his office, I immediately felt well, and the bleeding stopped.

I realized that I was not ready to become a mother. I wanted to remain in New York and continue progressing the experiments that I felt were more and more interesting. I thought of having an abortion, although it might have been too late. Takis thought I should have the baby: 'We can send him to my mother in Athens to grow up with the goats.' I argued that a child couldn't grow up without parents, but Takis countered that Oedipus had grown up without his parents and become great and wise.

I could have argued that the shepherd and his wife were parents, but I didn't think Oedipus was a great example. I agreed to keep the baby but decided that my parents would make better carers. Takis insisted that we had to get married, mainly because he'd had so much trouble with his first child, Anna, the daughter of the British painter Sheila Fell.

I rang my father to tell him that I was pregnant and that we were going to get married. His reaction was, 'Why? You don't need to get married. I will look after your child.' My father was probably right. Takis's idea of marriage was to make sure he had the legal rights of parenthood. He had no intention of behaving like a father, let alone a husband. I never asked why Sheila had not allowed him to see their daughter until she was nearly nine. Perhaps, he simply hadn't bothered to see her. Takis said that, whatever happened, we needed to be free spirits, and I wanted nothing more. He told me to shine like the sun. I liked the idea and didn't analyse its meaning. I was caught between Takis and my father. The latter would have liked nothing better than for me to live with him, to be a kind of ersatz father to my baby. Takis was happy for me to have his baby but wasn't offering a moment of his time. With the boundless energy and carelessness of youth I decided I would manage and went ahead with both pregnancy and marriage.

We were married in a green room in downtown Manhattan's dreary town hall, by a man who mouthed the traditional words without the slightest empathy or interest. We had two witnesses, my flat-mate Merriman and my father's lawyer, who afterwards took us all out for an excellent steak. I had to smother my hysterical giggles throughout the farcical five-dollar ceremony. Takis took it very seriously and was insulted when he came across a list in my notebook, where 'get married' shared a page with 'buy more Perspex, get oranges'. Half amused, half hurt, he asked, 'Who do you think you are, Greta Garbo?' Obviously, I should have been. My father had urged me to go to drama school, adding that he would introduce me to Jack Warner, with whom he often played chemin de fer. But I chose to be an artist.

Having spent all of September in New York, Takis left for Paris two days after our marriage. I would not see him again until after the birth of my son.

On Becoming a Mother

Now that I was carrying another life inside me, I planned to be more careful. Although I didn't think very much about being pregnant, I knew that a pregnant woman artist would not be taken seriously. Motherhood did not exude a professional aroma. To be an artist took total dedication, which, it was thought, was nearly impossible for a woman, let alone a mother. My condition was a closely guarded secret I mentioned only to family, Merriman and a few close friends.

This first pregnancy felt like my body had been possessed, which is interesting in the light of the frequent accusations that young women suffered in medieval times of being possessed by demons. My body was possessed, but not by a demon. Instead, it was absorbed in the act of procreation, the development of another life. Despite being, at times, quite overcome by the changes my body experienced, I kept working right through the early stages of my pregnancy without thinking very much about it. By chance, I met Deborah Lane, one of the brightest students in Solebury, now married and pregnant with her first child. I was amazed at her preoccupation with her unborn child. She spoke of nothing else. She read Dr Spock religiously and anxiously followed all his advice. What, I wondered, had happened to her ambitions, her poetry? I, on the other hand, didn't give it a second thought. I continued as if I didn't have tender, swelling breasts and a slowly growing foetus in my belly. There was no ultrasound, no way to check for aberrations or gender. My gynaecologist simply felt my belly and said, 'Healthy baby, going to be very tall. Has big feet!'

There's a note in my diary for a letter to Takis:

I have never felt so alive and powerful, as in these last months since you left. My mind is very quick and all my thoughts creative. It is as if I am using the extraordinary powers of the growing life inside me, instead of it sapping my life and energy. It is really exciting!

I found a small triangular studio above a Greek luncheonette on the corner of Broome and West Broadway. Its tall windows on two sides gave me plenty of light. Although hot in summer and freezing in winter, I loved it. I enjoyed the short walk from the apartment every morning and night. What is now known as SoHo, the area between Houston and Canal, was then mainly warehouses and small industrial units. These small companies had started moving out of Manhattan, making room for artists to take over the empty spaces, still relatively cheap to rent. On Greene Street, there was a cooperative engineering shop, full of machines used by artists. They were all men and, although curious about the facilities, I didn't feel welcome to use them. Instead, I went to a New Jersey factory producing acrylic polymers. They may have produced Plexiglass, but I was mainly interested in the material's liquid state. Having had health problems from burning Tefonstift, I wanted to research the toxicity of this new material. I had started using liquid acrylic that I bought in small bottles from Industrial Plastics, and

I planned to buy a ten-gallon drum. I was told that it was not toxic, but it was highly inflammable. I heated my studio with an open paraffin burner. Teflon, they told me, would have killed me in less than a minute, exploding my bronchi, so the Tefonstift did not contain Teflon or, if it did, only in negligible quantities.

Instead of the threads of extruded plastic that constituted *Fire Lines*, doubling into a labyrinth of vibrating lines once I had sprayed the back of the Perspex sheets white, I now let drops and splashes of clear acrylic polymer fall on to the surface. I continued to spray the back white, having noticed that the reflections and shadows were of great interest and brought the whole tableau to life, giving it a richness that the single surface layer didn't have. With *Fire Lines*, it was much clearer; the lines, when doubled by their shadows, appeared to move as one looked at the work from different angles. Using polymer, the reflections were luminous against the white background and biomorphic. It was a whole new world.

I had bought aniline dyes and I tried introducing delicate transparent colour. When the clear polymer dried it was almost impossible to see it on the surface of the Perspex sheet. Only the reflection was visible, when lit with a bright direct light. My studio was very sunny, and the reflections were intricate and beautiful. When I used a small amount of aniline dye, the soft pastel reflections were interesting, but I didn't like seeing the coloured polymer on the surface. I was only interested in reflections and shadows. I wondered how I could make coloured reflections visible, without seeing the pigmented polymer that cast them. How to achieve invisible colour?

My Israeli cousin Gabi Segall had been accepted to MIT, majoring in physics. I wrote and asked him whether he might be able to solve my problem. He invited me to visit. Gabi introduced me to his professor as his experimental artist cousin. They had already discussed my problem and they'd found it interesting enough to give it some thought and had figured out a way to see reflections without seeing their source. The theoretical solution was to display the work in a dark room, using a projector with Polaroid lenses to cut out the colour. But, I asked, if it removed the surface colour, wouldn't it also take out the reflected colour? They replied that I would need to experiment to see if I could avoid that.

Back in New York, I bought Polaroid lenses and experimented with them, but I soon felt that the result was not worth the complex production required. I wanted to discover a more straightforward, purer path.

Carrying on as normal, concentrating on my experiments with plastic, works that appeared so close to the ephemeral, almost invisible play of light and shadows, visiting galleries with Paul Cummings, meeting with Juliet, I didn't notice the far from subtle changes in my body, the swelling of my breasts and the slow, hard enlarging of my abdomen. I didn't give these changes a thought, instead recording my favourite vinyl records on tape and writing long letters to Takis. To which he responded with loving, anxious letters in his third-grade English. Was I looking after myself, not smoking too much and getting enough sleep? He was concerned but he wasn't there.

As my body changed, so did my name, but Liliane Lijn appeared to confuse. For a start, no one could pronounce Lijn and, to complicate matters, on a romantic whim after our marriage I had put Takis's last name, Vassilakis, on my passport. Perhaps this gave me the feeling that I was indeed married.

When my pregnancy could no longer be hidden, I fled to Florida, where I lived in a small room a few doors down from my mother and André's apartment, only a short walk to the beach. My mother rented this room from her neighbour, a Florida born-and-bred white family. Their thin, blonde daughter, younger than me, was also pregnant and had her baby before I left. They told us proudly that it had simply popped out, in under an hour, with hardly any labour. If they hadn't told us, we'd never have known she was pregnant.

I lived in a bathing suit or a light loose dress. In the morning, I ambled over to my mother's apartment for a delicious breakfast. Living with André had brought about many positive changes in my mother. She had learned how to touch type, had become an excellent cook and crocheted exquisite suits and coats. She accompanied me to the beach, terrified by my diving into the large breakers or swimming out a bit too far, where, she claimed, there were sharks.

Fort Lauderdale in 1962 was a small fishing

village on the beach with an inland, nondescript town centre. Segregation was officially over, but people of colour were visible only in menial jobs or in a separate quarter of town, where one was advised not to go. The seafront seemed to be out of bounds for them, and their exclusion and the sense of oppression was depressing.

At night I would lie awake long hours, feeling my body change. As my belly grew and I could feel my child moving inside, his feet poking out, I allowed myself to slide into the 'heat and the opulence of matter'.* I became flesh, oozing gelatinous membranes and orifices, protruding tits and slithery cunt. Pregnant woman, hot desiring body alone in my small bed, feeling that I was sex, huge and all-engulfing sex, without a man, without fulfilment.

My mind was clear, even if, at times, it disappeared into my body as into a mountain of throbbing flesh. I kept myself busy reading and sketching. I taught myself Greek by reading Aristophanes' plays, using a dictionary to translate the words. I had difficulty finding some of the words so, discovering there was a young Greek living next door, I

* From *Crossing Map*, Liliane Lijn, 1983.

went to meet him and asked if he would translate the missing words. He blushed and said that he couldn't utter them to a woman in my condition. He finally gave in, and I was initiated into the mysteries of Greek gay pornography.

Warm weather was so predictably regular, it was easy to forget that the New York sidewalks were piled high with freezing snow and ice. I began to take the sun shining on the glittering salty sea for granted. Then we had a hurricane. During the worst of it we stayed huddled indoors. When the violence abated, there was great excitement on the street. Our neighbours were running towards the beach, carrying pails and bins, and waved to us to come along. We grabbed a plastic pail and ran with them to the seafront. The water was boiling and dark with the massed bodies of a million small mackerel. Further out, five or six pelicans swam in a sweeping semi-circle, steadily pushing the shoal of fish towards the beach, where a line of people were waiting with their bins and their pails. When they came close enough, the water literally black with fish, we scooped up a pailful. We were much impressed by the pelicans' teamwork and thankful for our excellent dinner.

*

At the beginning of April, I was back in New York. It was time to give birth, but my baby thought otherwise, and I felt more and more uncomfortable. My gynaecologist said it might be best to induce labour. I hadn't read any books about pregnancy or childbirth and was happy to come into hospital on the 17th. I couldn't wait to be free of the suffocating weight and the painful leg cramps, to get back to my normal body. I called my mother to tell her I was going into hospital and, accompanied by Merriman, went in on the appointed morning.

I was reading Vance Packard's *The Status Seekers* and took the book with me. The doctor wasn't there, so I lay down reading, completely unconcerned. Even after he arrived and gave me the pills to induce labour, I kept reading, as if nothing was happening. Then he decided it wasn't moving quickly enough and he would have to break my amniotic membrane. That done, everything moved very quickly; contractions came so fast that one nurse thought she saw the head and ran out of the room to fetch the doctor. The violence of the contractions and the extreme pain was more than I could bear. I started crying out and swearing, distressing the nurses. I was alone, without any comfort or support. The nurses lifted my feet and tied them into metal stirrups, legs wide open. I frantically tried to prevent this, so they strapped my arms to my sides and the doctor covered my face with a mask, telling me to breathe deeply.

I woke in a large, darkened room with five other women. The woman in front of me was moaning and crying. She had just had a Caesarean and the nurse kept asking her to cough to get the phlegm out of her lungs, but it was obvious that coughing was acutely painful. Everyone had their babies to hold and suckle. I felt fine, but where was my baby? I was told he was on a separate floor. For the first two days after the birth, they wouldn't allow me to see him, and I began to worry that something was wrong.

My mother arrived with a pretty, flowery nightie and fruit. My friend Juliet came with her younger sister, Lola, and Merriman visited with flowers and chocolates. But I still hadn't seen my child. Finally, I was allowed upstairs to visit him and peered at the tiny being through a large plate-glass wall. We were segregated. My baby was in the luxury area, while I was lying on a lower floor in an overcrowded ward.

My father had paid for a private room but, until one became available, my son was nursed upstairs, while I remained below.

My father rang to congratulate me, bursting with pride and joy. I had to take his call standing at a payphone in the hallway. 'Your cousin Toli in Tel Aviv also had a son a few months ago and he named him Joseph after your grandfather. You must do the same and name your son after his grandfather.'

'What was his name?' I asked.

'Itshak.'

I thought of the German word *hacken* that I knew meant to hack, to chop, and I didn't like the feeling. Isaak was too biblical, too patriarchal. I told him that I would have to think about it. Almost immediately afterwards, Takis rang, excited that I had given birth to a boy. He was in Milan for an exhibition. He said that a woman had told him he would have a son, who would be as beautiful as a god. Takis told me that my father had managed to contact him, when it should have been the other way around. I felt that the two men in my life were claiming ownership from afar. I told Takis about my father's idea for a name. I thought he agreed with me, but then he told me that boys had to take their name from their father's family: 'We can name him after my father, Athanasios.'

I was a prisoner of the patriarchy, caught between these two men I loved, but from whose shackles I yearned to be free. I had no other name for the little sleeping creature, so I gratefully accepted Athanasios, the Immortal, as a small victory over my father. My father, who had paid for me to be in a deluxe room, who proudly telegraphed his friends and business colleagues worldwide. My room overflowed with their flowers and notes of congratulation in several languages. He had even persuaded Takis to fly to New York at his expense. I spent ten days in hospital, most of them in a large room overlooking the East River, learning to bottle-feed my baby because the gynaecologist had told me that breastfeeding would ruin the shape of my breasts and that formula milk was just as good – and easier, since someone else could feed him. It all seemed logical and so my first encounter with motherhood was anything but natural.

When I left the hospital with my small son, I found that Merriman had moved out of the apartment so that my mother could stay there to help me. A few days later, my father came to see his grandson, looking very worn, his face furrowed by deep lines. A friend of his came to take photographs by candlelight: of me holding my baby; of my mother and her mother either side of me; of my father with the tiny creature cradled in his large arms. He accepted his grandson's Greek name, although he told me that this would offend my cousin and his family, and suggested I find a nanny.

A week later, Takis arrived. It was strange, after six months, to see him again. After all the letters of love and longing, and my fantasies of being with him and our child, the reality of his arrival was almost an interruption. He didn't fit well into the scene of recent birth, of parenting. He was restless from the start, although he held his infant son for a moment and smiled at him. We called him Thanos. He was beautiful, but he cried and cried, and we didn't know what to do.

Takis suggested that we leave him with my mother and go to meet Gregory at the Blue Note. He promised we wouldn't stay very late. I felt fragile, and the club's loud music and cigarette smoke disturbed me, although I was glad to see

Gregory, who congratulated both of us warmly. He announced that he had a new wealthy girl-friend, whom Takis wanted to check out, but she wasn't coming until later. After a couple of hours, I began to feel tired and wanted to leave, but Takis insisted on staying to meet Gregory's new friend: 'I can't break things. I must see them through to the end.' He put me into a taxi. I felt very hurt that he couldn't change his habits, that I and his baby son were less important to him than Corso's gossip or his new girl, that he preferred to continue drinking and smoking dope.

Family. Children. Takis wasn't interested. I didn't realize then just how much he missed out on. I was surprised at the intense feelings of tenderness I felt towards the small new being who was now in my care. They came in a sudden rush the first time I held him, feeding him with a bottle supplied by the hospital nurse, gazing at his miraculously perfect body with its extra-large feet, augurs of future height and glory.

One month after Thanos's birth, I landed in Geneva with Maureen, my Irish nanny. I found her through a New York agency when, desperate at my inability to cope with sleepless nights and diapers, I took my father's advice. Maureen's last job had been with a Palm Beach family, friends of the Kennedys. Nevertheless, when I explained that I was an artist and the situation would be very different, much less luxurious but we would travel, she seemed very happy to take the position. As soon as she arrived, she took complete control. She had an extraordinary way with babies. Thanos felt safe and happy in her hands. There is a photo of us arriving, taken from the airport terrace where people awaited friends and relatives. We're both looking up: I'm wearing a wide-brimmed black hat that frames my very young face; Maureen, her face long and thin, cradles in her arms a small bundle.

I was very tired after the long flight and would have liked to sleep, but my father had planned a welcome party. His large living room was filled with toys and people. How could I spoil his intense pleasure? He'd bought a large cot with a lacy canopy fit for a prince. He'd laid on food and drink, and made a speech. Every one of his friends wanted to ply me with questions about my plans. How did I feel now that I was a mother? Where was my husband? Would I still make art? It was endless and unanswerable. I escaped into the small room where Thanos slept, blissfully unaware of the commotion his arrival had created. I stood in the calm of that room, a little envious of his newness, of the yet undetermined potential that was his.

A Centre for World Peace in Cyprus

In June, after a short stay in Venice, Takis and I took a boat to meet Caresse Crosby in Cyprus, with her old friend Buckminster Fuller and President Archbishop Makarios, to discuss the building of a Centre for World Peace. Bucky had agreed to build a dome to house the centre, and Takis and I were to be the first artist citizens. Caresse imagined her centre as an autonomous state within a country. Two years earlier, she had tried to establish it in Delphi and had very nearly succeeded. The Greek government, however, had not liked the idea of an independent domain within its borders. Caresse thought that Makarios would be a freer spirit.

I had left little Thanos with my father, in Maureen's excellent care, since there was no question of

Takis playing daddy and, after so many months of separation, we wanted to spend time together. It was strange to part from my barely two-month-old child. I felt as if I'd left a part of myself behind.

In our cabin, I was mesmerized by reflections from the droplets of water that kept forming and reforming on the porthole as the waves splashed against the side of the boat. I sketched this as something I might be able to develop. As the air currents altered their form, the luminous drops threw flares of light across the porthole; new drops splashed on the glass and spread, erasing earlier ones. I wanted to create a work that would give the same sensation of luminosity and becoming, evanescence, dissolution and renewal.

The boat stopped in Athens and we visited Takis's family for the afternoon. Returning to the boat, we received a telegram that the meeting was postponed, due to urgent political problems on the island. What a disappointment, not only because of the collaboration with Buckminster Fuller, but also because I was looking forward to seeing Caresse again. I felt she considered me a spiritual daughter. She'd visited me in New York after an operation about which she refused to talk, saying that death did not worry her because she was a humanist. She encouraged me to write and to concentrate on making art. Her own extraordinary life was an inspiration and a powerful influence on me as an example of a brilliantly inventive individual and my unforgettable mentor. I didn't think that 'urgent political problems' were the main cause of the cancellation. It was more probable that Makarios had realized the implications of the Centre and had decided to back out. How disappointed Caresse must have been.

We cancelled our trip to Cyprus and decided to remain in Athens. Takis hadn't seen his family for some years because the last time he'd visited he claimed they'd stripped him of everything but the clothes on his back. I had already met his mother, his sister Tita and, briefly, his wild brother Vassilis, whose fiancée already lived in his mother's house, drifting around in her nightie. Now I met brother Giorgos, who appeared to be more refined, and his two other sisters, Lilika and Titika, whom I would get to know better in the coming years. Takis took me to Attica, to show me the land his father had cultivated before the arrival of the refugees from Turkey in the 1920s. As a boy, he'd loved to walk its deep ravines, where water used to flow and flowering plants flourished. He described it in such nostalgic detail, but on arrival the ravines were dry, the bare cracked earth stony. People used them as garbage dumps. We walked in silent mourning.

But there were other places: a large bare hill with a few ramshackle houses at its base. Takis had often walked there since one could see all Athens, the Parthenon and the sea beyond. Once at the top, we saw that the other side was cultivated and green. Takis said the farmers who ploughed that land came from the village of Menidi, and he wanted to take me there for lunch to try the local speciality, a soup with sheep's guts that he said was the farmer's breakfast. They also had *kokoretse*, a long sausage of sheep's innards rotating on an outdoor spit. The soup revolted me, but to his delight I liked the *kokoretse*. When we were alone, he was very attentive, hoping that I would like the same foods he did, the ones that brought back memories, concerned that I would not be able to face the discomforts of 'Life with Takis'. The hill was called Gero Vouno or 'Old Mountain'. Takis said it was a special place because the kings of Acharnon were buried there. It was important to him that his father had once owned this land and I could see that he wanted to claim it back. He spoke excitedly of buying some land at the top. We would leave the grimy cities behind and live on this luminous hill. We could build an observatory and watch the stars. I immediately agreed. I loved its ancient soft form and bare ochre earth, the shimmering white city on one side and the deep green on the other. It was a dream, but we felt we had not come to Greece in vain. We would create something here.

I had sold my green sports car in New York, and practical Giorgos helped us rent a car. We drove to Delphi and across to the Peloponnese, to Corinth, Mycenae and Argos.

In Delphi, we visited the temples, theatre and stadium in the midday heat and walked around naked, because no one else came there at that hour. We photographed each other, the large ancient marble slabs, and the much smaller marble paving of the recently built paths. In his opinion, the contemporary paving was evidence of the decadence of our culture, moving irrevocably away from an understanding of matter. His arguments impressed me and had a lasting influence on my own ideas about how our culture had moved from an attachment to matter to a reliance on images, progressing from those to digital data for information, communication and understanding reality. Takis was nostalgic for the matter-based world. As artists, we both had a love of materials and an interest in how they were used. He would point out a particularly large paving slab and the way it was connected to the adjacent stone, saying the ancient Greeks built a marble avenue, whereas modern Greek architects were building a poor image of an avenue with their small pieces of stone.

Takis's sister Tita was married to Thanasis Calogeresis, a lawyer who sorted out all of Aristotle Onassis's Greek land deals. He was involved in building a hotel in Agiou Nikolaos in Crete and invited us to go there for a week. We were driven to Knossos, where archaeological digs were ongoing. They'd begun piecing together an ancient mural and, even though I had studied archaeology, I wondered how they managed to put the fragments together. There were such enormous gaps to fill with one's imagination.

Tita thought Takis might want to buy some land near the plots they had bought. We drove through plantations of bananas and pineapples, plants that I had never seen before. It was incredibly hot, and I felt dizzy, listening constantly to a language I couldn't understand. In Agiou Nikolaos, Takis took me to a typical Cretan taverna, where we sat on a shady terrace, drinking ouzo with meze. He told me that his father's side of the family originally came from Crete. I felt stronger being able to bathe in the sea, but Takis started feeling pain in his lower back and began to see blood in his urine. We couldn't find a doctor so, in desperation, I drove him to the nearest hospital. We arrived to find a long line of miserable people standing outside under the sweltering sun. We learned that many of them — with broken arms, high fevers, sick babies — had walked for miles and might have to wait for days, without food or even water. We didn't have to wait long because we were well connected and could pay. Takis was taken to a bare room and put to bed. They hardly seemed to have the simplest necessities. No one came to see him, and he lay there moaning in pain, telling me to leave. I tried to phone Tita, who was now back in Athens, for help. I wanted her to call the hospital and use Thanasis's influence to make something happen. I wasn't sure what Takis might have or how serious it could be and began to worry that he might die. Finally, a doctor came and examined Takis and told me that he had a big stone in his kidney. They hoped that by drinking a lot of liquid the stone would be ejected. Takis was there for three painful days, but finally the stone was pissed out and we left Crete.

After convincing myself that Thanos would be well looked after, living with my father in Geneva, I returned to New York, to my studio and the shared apartment on King Street.

Through the autumn, I lived in a ferment of ideas that I immediately developed into new works, while I continually met people who either helped me make work or were interested in what I was creating.

In my studio on Broome and West Broadway, I worked with the clear viscous acrylic monomer that I splattered first across a sheet of Perspex and then on Perspex cylinders, sprayed white inside with the transparent polymer splashed or dripped on the outsides. I wanted them to rotate so that the reflections moved, hoping they'd resemble what I'd seen on our cabin portholes during our crossing from Venice to Athens. At first, I thought of fixing the cylinders behind a stretched canvas through which one saw the moving, changing reflections. I made two, the first a black one, about 80 cm x 60 cm, with one comparatively small window at its centre. Its surface was not flat, because the structure that held the cylinder in place pushed the canvas outwards. The second work used a larger canvas and two vertical cylinders, placed apart and at different heights. I painted the canvas ochre, but the monochrome colour looked dead and flat. I painted the surface over and over, underpainting with a different colour, finally achieving a rich, vibrant surface. These were my first motorized kinetic works.

Looking back, I ask myself why I made the kinetic reflections so small a part of the whole. I think I wanted to capture the feeling of peering through a small window; also, to make them larger would have been technically difficult. Takis was in Paris, and I cannot think who might have helped me with my first venture into the mechanics of motion. He must have encouraged and advised in our frequent correspondence. Cross-Atlantic telephone communication was still expensive and needed an operator, so we constantly wrote each other letters.

I had an even more ambitious idea for the third work. I wanted the mechanism to be visible and the cylinder to appear like a totem in a wooden-sided glass case. I wasn't sure how to go about making this. Around then, I met a young man on the street in the village who told me, after we had been chatting for a while, that he didn't know where he would sleep that night. I immediately invited him to stay the night with Merriman and me. He had graduated from college but had decided to become a carpenter. I was delighted to hear that, since I hoped he would make the case for my new work. The next day, he asked me how I could invite a man I didn't know to sleep over in our apartment.

I continued to make more *Cuttings* and *Drillings*, drilling into thick blocks of Perspex. Once I had drilled holes into but not through a clear Perspex block, I painted the drilled side white. The holes, seen from the opposite side, now looked like solid cylindrical forms, casting shadows against the white background. I tried pouring acetic acid into the holes and bashing them with a screwdriver and hammer. That caused interesting internal crazing and even bubbles at the ends of the holes. I then tried mixing aniline dyes with the acid to colour the holes. I was diffident about using colour and only made a few works with the dyes.

Among those who visited my studio were Nikos Callas and his wife, Lolia. Nikos was a Greek poet, art historian and critic, tall, wiry and always slightly bent, his face dominated by his expressive eyebrows; Lolia, smaller and stockier, seemed to be his adviser. They were curious about my work and looked carefully at the different pieces. We discussed the New York art scene and whether my work might interest any galleries. Nikos's primary interest was surrealism, and he was a friend of Alexander Iolas, through whom he had met Takis. He suggested the Staempfli Gallery, on the corner of 77th and Madison, because they worked with two kinetic artists, Tinguely and George Ricky. George Staempfli, originally Swiss, knew Nikos and respected his opinion, and Nikos arranged for him to visit my studio. I was nervous about Staempfli's visit and cleaned my studio to make sure he could see the work. He came with Nikos and Lolia, and decided to take one of my polymer *Reflection* works on consignment.

Invited to the opening of his next exhibition, I was thrilled to see my pristine work next to a Giacometti drawing. Spotlit, the reflections and shadowy outlines of the amorphous shapes of clear and slightly yellow polymer seemed to glitter. As I was admiring it, Nikos introduced me to an older man, an important collector. Dan Weitzmann had said he wanted to meet the maker of such a pure work of art. He invited us to come to his house after the opening. The other person invited was the Venezuelan artist Marisol, whose work I was unfamiliar with. Weitzmann had just acquired one of her large figure sculptures and wanted her to see how he had displayed it. His apartment was spacious and decorated in a minimalist style that emphasized his collection of American abstract expressionist and colour field painters, Morris Louis, Clyfford Still, de Kooning, Ad Reinhardt and Helen Frankenthaler. Marisol's figure was carved and painted wood – it was the first time I had seen one and it looked powerful among the work of so many important male artists. Marisol was beautiful and confident, and spoke briefly in a quiet voice, only when asked a question. Her silent manner made me feel uncomfortable, probably because I was exactly the opposite. Before we left, Dan arranged to visit my studio.

During Dan's visit, we discussed my works. He preferred the less intensely coloured works, saying the colour distracted from the pure essence of the clear reflections. The polymer reflections were biomorphic, like protozoa or some early life form one might see under a microscope. I was hoping he would buy a work but was completely unprepared when he asked me for a price. I must have quoted too high a figure, since he hesitated, saying he wanted to see where I would go next.

I felt uncomfortable when he then invited me to dinner. When he ordered a nice wine, I told him that I didn't drink. In fact, I hardly ever drank wine in those days. I only learned to like it after living in Greece, because I liked the taste of retsina. He looked at me as if I didn't quite make the grade and said, 'Don't you appreciate the nice things in life?' I wondered whether his interest in my pure art had slithered into a less pure interest in the young artist.

In Takis speak, Dan was an A – most collectors were. An A was wealthy, powerful, both able and willing to exploit others. Most artists were Bs, as were peasants and the working class. Wealthy As bribed artists with promises of fame and money to forget their dreams of freedom and equality, to make their art marketable and increase their investment value. According to Takis, artists in the West were paid off with success to stop exploring and to enter the 'real world'. In more authoritarian countries, the Eastern bloc or Communist China, artists were simply imprisoned or killed. Pure Bs were considered a danger to social equilibrium.

Sitting opposite Dan, in the expensive restaurant to which he had so generously invited me, I saw him metamorphose into a cynical, hardhearted A, a puritanical workaholic or a potential gynophobic seducer. Under his critical cool blue eyes, I felt vulnerable, naked, without artifice or the taught mannerisms that protect from disturbing intrusions. I did not have the style or the banter to know how to behave with an important collector, who could be of such help to my career. Naturally, since I did not have a 'career'; nor did I think about my work in those terms. It was my life, the air I breathed. I had no other clear identity and yet it was still in its infancy, so how could I defend my Self?

After my return to Paris, Dan sent me a long encouraging letter, making me realize I had misjudged him. I wrote back, but our correspondence eventually petered out.

I became friends with Canadian sculptor

Robert Murray, who was only three years older, but so much more organized and successful. He came to my studio, photographed my works, showed me his portfolio, and made me realize how amateurish I was. Perhaps because I had not been to art school, had not learned that it was necessary to have slides of one's works, how to approach galleries, to compare notes with other artists of my age. But Robert showed me what was necessary, giving me a glimpse of the usual way a young artist developed both their work and their ego. Perhaps he had had a more normal, more socially integrated upbringing, and at art school had learned to think of himself as an artist. Robert helped me document my works and made me aware that I needed to organize myself.

He was married to a quiet woman, whom I didn't get to know, even when they invited me to a party in their loft. There were several interesting people there and I was attracted to a large, humorous man I remember only as Max. There was a discussion about thinking when I insisted that my best thoughts were not conscious. There was a lot of argument about this, since most people believed that only conscious thoughts could be qualified as real thinking. Max offered to take me home and we ended up sleeping together. He had a soft coat of black hair on his back, more hair than I had ever seen on a man. He was gentle, cuddly and smart. He told me I had a perfect body as I preened in front of the mirror. What had impressed him was that when I stood up my skirt had lifted, showing my ass, and I had simply flicked it down and walked away. Some years later, I heard that he was the head of New York Public Radio.

In October 1962, Alexander Iolas invited me to the opening of a Niki de Saint Phalle exhibition, during which Niki shot paint pellets at a target in a dramatic, well-attended performance. She was ten years older than me, glamorous and successful. At a subsequent visit to her exhibition, I saw Iolas walk past a large painting covered with plastic prehistoric reptiles and, with an expression of revulsion, rip one off the canvas. Years later, Takis said that Iolas showed Niki because he was supported by her parents' bank. I thought that was unfair, since I'd heard that Tinguely had refused to exhibit if Iolas didn't also work with Niki.

Staempfli sent me a thoughtful letter, in which

he 'reluctantly came to the conclusion' that he 'would not like to take [my works] on at that time'. He explained that, although he was fascinated by my idea and by some of my work, he thought that I 'might soon discover even better ways of using your idea'. The accent, at that moment, was still too much on 'intellectual concepts'. He did ask to be shown new work 'from time to time' and, had I remained in New York, no doubt I would have followed up on that. Somehow, rejection, no matter how nicely phrased, is always felt as rejection, and I never did ask George Staempfli to view my work again.

Mrs Thibaut and Marilyn Fischbach found my work interesting and asked me to consign work to them for a group exhibition. This was in the early years of their gallery, where they later hosted Eva Hesse's first solo exhibition and, in 1966, the important Eccentric Abstraction exhibition, curated by Lucy Lippard. My definitive return to Paris towards the end of 1962 interrupted that relationship when it was too fresh and fragile to easily pick up again. Marilyn visited me in London in the late 1980s and told me that, had I stayed in New York, I would now have been an internationally famous artist. It was also what my friend Paul Cummings, curator of drawings at the Whitney and founder of *The Drawing Magazine*, kept telling me: 'You need to live in the Big Apple, Liliane. That is where it is happening.' I would hear that over and over again.

Back to Europe

Living alone in New York was empowering and I felt a great sense of freedom, but those I loved most were far from me. It seemed crazy that Thanos was with my father in Geneva, looked after by Maureen, Takis was in Paris and I was in New York. I was torn between my longing to be with them and my independent, creative life. I knew Takis would never settle down, but I reasoned that if I lived in Paris, at least I wouldn't be so far from my son and could visit him frequently. Once my mind was made up, I shipped all my works and materials, my books and records to a storage my father had in Geneva. I wasn't sure where I would be living in Paris.

Takis was living at the Hôtel La Louisiane and said he'd take a separate room for me. As independent free spirits, we should not live as a mean little couple. He said he had missed me terribly and was so happy to see me. Then he told me about Nazli, a beautiful English poet who had fallen in love with him.

'She has no ego. I fucked her but that's unimportant. I have told her about you, and she wants to meet you. I'm sure you will become friends.' I wasn't sure I wanted to meet her. I felt jealous, not just that he'd fucked her but that she was beautiful and that she'd fallen in love with him.

Nazli Nour's father, a miniature portrait painter at the Egyptian court, had married a French woman and they'd come to England, where Nazli was born. In 1958, Nazli wrote and directed the film *Alone with the Monsters*, a psychological study of people's unconscious cruelty towards those who appear different, which won a prize that allowed her to go to Poland to work with the famous Polish director Andrzej Wajda. On her way to Warsaw, Nazli stopped in Paris and met Takis, William Burroughs and the poets living at the Beat Hotel. She fell in love with Takis and never went to Warsaw. When I first met her, I was struck by her beautiful, lash-veiled violet eyes, sensual lips and buxom body, all so different from my boyish appearance. I could see why Takis had felt attracted to her, but surprisingly I didn't feel jealous. As he said, she was open, egoless and amoral. There was something childlike about her spontaneity and candid behaviour. She wrote long poems and painted watercolours, similar to animations, that she sold in the cafés around Saint-Germain. Nazli had a four-year-old son, Juba, possibly the result of a rape in London. She told me that when she reported the assault to the police, they accused her of prostitution. We met most days. Takis suggested the three of us sleep together to extinguish jealousy. I felt uncomfortable but curious, and Nazli agreed. My attention was focused more on her than on him. Takis wanted me to suck her nipples. Nazli's large soft breasts enveloped my face, suffocating me. Neither Nazli nor I derived much sexual pleasure from the experience.

In April I travelled to Lugano, where Thanos was staying with my mother. It was his first birthday, and he proudly showed me that he could walk. Nanny Maureen was with him but was planning to leave, since she didn't like being with my mother. Instead, my mother found an Italian nanny, Luisa, dark-haired, thin and nervous, but wonderful with

Thanos, who became very attached to her. My parents competed for the privilege of looking after Thanos, and I exploited that to persuade my mother to follow my instructions for Thanos, such as not feeding him sweets, and to make my father behave with me.

My father was still unhappy about my relationship with Takis. In one outburst, he claimed that he had investigated Takis and knew he was a criminal. 'I'll put him in jail,' he threatened. 'Why do you believe in him and that Greek, who says he can draw water from the earth?' Juliet thought my father was mad to accuse Takis of being a criminal and often told me so, and at times he did behave irrationally, but he was also supportive and very generous. His constant complaints about my life tortured me with feelings of guilt, particularly in relation to Thanos, although he never spoke about him, simply saying that I was wasting time with art, Takis and his Greek friends, who had nothing to give me; that I would be so much better off living in Geneva and getting a degree in literature or philosophy. It was useless trying to defend myself; instead I bought clothes, sometimes expensive couture. I sent him the bill and he'd simply say, 'She's her father's girl,' meaning that I had expensive tastes. He had any number of much younger girl-friends. Tonia, about ten years older than me, had won the French figure-skating title, then became an actress, and then Alain Delon's manager. She told me that, as an actress, being screwed was the rule, and she was fed up with men taking advantage. A girlfriend had taught her how to get even. On a first date you tested the man to see if he was a spender by asking him to buy something silly but expensive, like a huge fluffy toy. This had to be done at the right frivolous moment. If he bought it, he passed the test and would be good for a lot more. You promised but never slept with your mark. Tonia became addicted to this perversion, until she met Delon, who supported her, making her his manager. I asked whether she had conned my father. She just laughed, said she wasn't into that any more, and anyway, she loved him.

Takis had bought a maid's room on the fifth floor of a building on the rue Saint-André des Arts for a studio. It was long and narrow with a window at one end, a workbench along one wall, shelves on the other, a narrow cot and a sink. A shared Turkish toilet was on the next floor landing, with neither electric light nor toilet paper, instead a candle and newsprint on a nail. At some point I lived there, since I remember going to friends' for showers. Initially, I had worked in my hotel room, but Takis was happy to share his studio, if I didn't get in the way. Raymondos assisted him, and I helped them when there was a show to prepare.

I was not satisfied with the amorphous shapes that the polymer reflections took when I dripped the viscous liquid on the surface of clear acrylic sheets. I wanted to control the forms. I had started reading about light and I was more interested in visualizing photons than microscopic life forms that were easily seen. I'd discovered *Scientific American*, a magazine in which scientists published papers about quite varied subjects. Although not as academic as *Nature*, in the early 1960s it was a more serious journal than it is currently and published longer articles with more illustrations. Even when I didn't quite understand what I was reading, it was stimulating and inspiring. I thought that the language of science offered a new kind of poetry. Using a hypodermic syringe filled with liquid polymer, I could squeeze perfect, lens-shaped droplets on the clear sheets or blocks that I bought at the one place where one could buy plastics.

Finding materials in Paris was very different from New York, where I found them on Canal Street or the Yellow Pages. I loved the Yellow Pages, which opened a world of interesting companies, and where I always found whatever I needed. In Paris, one had to know where to go. All art materials were best bought behind Montparnasse, at Adam. Metals and plastics were sold in the well-stocked Weber store.

I placed coins on the surface of a clear block of acrylic to configure the patterns that I wanted to be seen as reflections and shadows. The result was geometric, but I would break the symmetry by taking out a coin here or there, until I felt the arrangement had become alive. I thought of that as 'breaking patterns'.

Then I would carefully squeeze the polymer on to the acrylic block. I bought thick blocks of Perspex, often up to 9 cm, because the reflections and shadows were cast at a deeper angle, allowing for more movement. Freshly applied, the droplets trembled and reflected light, like an array of early-morning dewdrops. When they dried and became part of the acrylic, they almost disappeared, only visible as reflections and shadows on the inner back surface because I painted the back of the blocks white. I felt that these were a great improvement on the more random biological patterns of my earlier works with liquid polymers.

I called these first works *Radiation Paintings*. They were wonderful seen in sunlight, but otherwise required a narrow-beam spotlight to see the luminous reflections. I wanted to find a way to make the reflections move independently from the viewer's movement. With Takis and Raymondos assisting, I designed and made a special spotlight that shone through a revolving lens. When I lit the acrylic block with my new projector, the convexity of the lens, which differed on each side, changed the direction of light, producing an unexpected and wonderful effect. Each dewdrop reflection appeared to double and triple, generating more reflections. I felt there was something atomic about these works, that I had captured photons of light, but I called them, quite modestly, *Echo-Lights*.

In the New York art world, pop art was big, and it was fast invading Paris. Yolanda and Michael Sonnabend were presenting pop art exhibitions in

European museums and in the new gallery they opened in 1962 on the Quai des Grands Augustins. Despite the skill and talent of so many pop artists, I could not relate to their work. In Paris, Denise René was showing works that I found interesting, although I thought the formal constructivist ethos of Vasarely and the Groupe de Recherches Visuelles too restrictive. I was attracted by the lyrical quality of Le Parc's works but felt they lacked the depth and power of Takis's work with the magnetic field.

Sinclair visited me whenever he was in Paris, and his encouragement was important. He lived in the Beat Hotel, almost opposite our little studio, so either with Takis or alone, I would drop by to share a smoke and take part in his mad tea rituals. He generously gave me a signed copy of *Minutes To Go*, the first anthology of cut-up poetry.* I loved the cut-up concept, the way in which it could instantly liberate you, unshackle the bonds of endeavour and

---

* 'Cut-ups', or the technique of cutting up and mixing two completely different texts together, was the idea of Brion Gysin, who suggested it to his friend William Burroughs.

the stiffness and silence that comes in front of the white page.

I also met the poet Harold Norse in the Beat Hotel. While I was in New York, he had seen and copied my *Sky Scrolls*, and exhibited them at a new basement gallery on the rue de Seine. It seemed that Takis even helped him frame and hang them, or so the rumour went. Takis told me Harold had stolen my idea and that the exhibition had sold quite well. He added that Harold's 'copies' weren't nearly as interesting as my originals. He had just used crayons as a resist brushed over with a coloured wash. I hadn't yet been offered a show. Harold, whose room was piled so high with medicines and herbs that you would have thought him a pharmacist, had you not known that he was a hypochondriac, never mentioned the show to me, nor did he ever tell me that he liked my drawings. But then, as Corso said, a poet needed to earn a living somehow.

At the Palais de la Découverte, the Paris Science Museum, I saw a beautiful object that was used in early optical experiments, investigating light interference and the paradox of the behaviour of light as both wave and particle. This paradox fascinated me, that something could assume opposite forms yet remain what it was. I was also interested in the writings of Buddhist disciplines, especially Japanese Zen, which spoke of instant enlightenment. I still had to learn that 'instant' did not have the same meaning as when applied to coffee. I needed to examine the concept of instant enlightenment more carefully to realize that what mattered was the preparation. Paradox played an important part in Zen and was the essence of the riddles, *koans*, given to young monks to aid meditation. *Echo-Lights* captured something of the photon paradox, in that the reflections were both points and flares.

The optics department at the Palais was full of fascinating displays; many nineteenth-century experiments were fashioned so beautifully that they looked more like art objects. Inspired, I decided to make my own experiment with light interference – more ambitious than the kinetic works I'd made in New York. It consisted of two drums, or cylinders, held horizontally and rotating in opposite directions. On their surface, I wanted to draw a series of straight and slightly oblique lines. I made some sketches and consulted Takis and Monsieur Papon, who owned a tiny shop on the rue du Sabot, stocked full of used motors and turntables. He sold me the motors I needed and some cylindrical metal drums.

My real discovery was Letraset in every kind of font, even arrows and lines.* To use it, one simply had to rub it on a surface. Raymondos helped me make *Le Vibrograph*. When the horizontal drums turned, the straight black lines on their surface seemed to curve and vibrate. There was also an aura of colour. As I sat and watched, it occurred to me that there might be similar vibrations were I to use words. Words were formed with letters and letters with lines. I became very excited by the equivalence between words and lines. Blurred words were lines in motion. Energy vibrations. And so was sound, the sound of the spoken word. I was not sure where to begin, but decided that the alphabet was a good start, and made a spinning drum using random Letraset letters. Then, I thought, I would cut up newspaper headlines for my next . . . *Poem Machine*. Tinguely had made machines that scribbled and drew. I would make machines to liberate the word. When Nazli saw the first Letraset alphabet drum,

* Letraset originally referred to sheets of transfer lettering used by graphic designers.

she immediately asked me to make her poems move. I told her I had thought of creating my own cut-ups

'Use my poems,' she insisted.

I told her they were too long, and I would have to edit them.

'Do whatever you like but put my poems on your drums. I want them to vibrate.'

Carl Laszlo, writer and publisher of Editions Panderma, bought a few *Cuttings*. He asked me to contribute to a large book in which many well-known artists would each have a page to create an original work. I must have made over a hundred small Plexiglass 'Radiations', without realizing just how invisible and easy to lose they were. To see anything, one had to detach the Plexiglass from the white piece of paper on which I had planted my signature and hold it in the light. I didn't have a feel for design. I was a visionary artist poet, which was why my work appealed to poets.

Takis and I would meet for coffee, always at the Old Navy's glassed-in terrace, where we waited to be joined by Minos or Raymondos, or other Greek artists. My friends had moved on while I was in New York. I saw Nazli often, while I worked on placing passages from her long poems on metal drums. I was introduced to Gaïte Frogé, who owned La Librairie Anglaise on the rue de Seine, a small stuffy bookshop where many Beat poets and artists congregated. Edwina Rubenstein, an American painter, had agreed to finance a gallery in Gaïte's basement. Edwina was independently wealthy and lived in the Marais with her two teenagers.

The gallery had opened while I was in New York and had already hosted some exhibitions, including the one of Harold Norse's gouaches. It was also there that Takis and Sinclair had held the *A Trials*, early performances that caused quite a stir. One trial accused William Burroughs of killing a pure B, his former wife Joan, in a drunken game of William Tell, by shooting an apple placed on her head. Burroughs was accused of being a Sly B, ready and willing to become an A. These denominations were part of Takis's and Sinclair's separation of people into different categories, depending on the purity of their heart and purpose.

Edwina asked me to exhibit in the basement of La Librairie Anglaise. I called the exhibition *Echo-Lights and Vibrographes*. The *Vibrograph* concept led straight to my earliest *Poem Machines* after the momentous realization that words were written with letters and letters were formed by lines. This influenced much of my subsequent practice, since I could exchange the spinning blurred words for oscillating lines on my later work with cones, and even the light columns, which I began in the late 1960s, partook of the same communicating line concept.

My father insisted on renting a house near the beach in Varkisa for a 'wonderful' family summer vacation for me, Takis and our one-year-old son. Takis was already in Athens when I arrived with a suitcase full of new dresses, bought during a stay in Geneva, where Thanos was once again living with my father.

There were pistachio trees in the back yard. It was very hot. At the local butcher, bleeding carcasses hung on great hooks in front of the shop. As he wrapped lamb chops in paper, the butcher offered me the animal's balls, adding in Greek that they were especially good for my husband. I didn't even know what they were and took them back to Takis, who laughed: 'Here they believe these will make me more of a man.'

We went to the beach. Bored, Takis sat on a towel smoking and played a little with his baby son. His family came to visit. Takis grumbled that we had landed in the most bourgeois part of Greece. I had wanted to go to an island, like Mykonos, but my mother had threatened that my father would have a heart attack if we went to such a remote place. Go to an island without doctors with a small child! Unthinkable! Takis spent a lot of time in Athens. All in all, Varkisa was not a success.

Back in Paris in September, I met Jean-Jacques again, who, familiar with the New York art scene, was creating happenings.* We spoke about Nina's horribly sudden death. He said he was organizing a happening in her memory, called *Pour Conjurer L'Esprit du Catastrophe*, and would I like to take part? I had been to several loft happenings in New York and diffidently agreed to be part of his. I wanted to commemorate my friend and I also felt that it would be a way of meeting more people. It took place in a film studio in Boulogne-Billancourt,

* A happening is a performance, event or situation art. The term was first used by Allan Kaprow during the 1950s.

with large paintings on the walls and a bathtub full of red water on a stage. The Icelandic painter Erro, whom I had known as Ferro, wore a body mask much like armour. Also performing were the Japanese artists Tetsumi and Hiroko Kudo. Tetsumi was dressed like a giant flapping penis. Beautiful Desirée swung quite naked in a hammock. A buxom blonde German woman and I were asked to strip to the waist and perform before a large crowd and the intrusive cameras of an aggressive and unexpected film crew, who were recording the event as part of a documentary on the youth of Europe, *Mondo Cane*. Jean-Jacques had interested the press and Pablo Volta photographed it for the Italian magazine *Le Ore*.

My mother, unaware that I was in *Mondo Cane*, saw the film with one of her Lugano friends on a trip to Milan. Embarrassed, shocked, secretly proud, she exclaimed, 'That's my daughter!' There I was, splashing about in a bath of blood, masked to appear as Kennedy (not long before he was assassinated), with the blonde and buxom Khrushchev beside me. Appearing almost naked was liberating. I was active, aggressive. I splashed blood at the cameras from my metaphorical bath and danced, holding the stuffed penis Kudo in my arms. Laughing, I carried a flag forward, quite unaware of what it symbolized. I was probably born to be a performer. Put me on a stage and I feel totally at home, loving and condescending to my audience. At times like these, I ask myself why I hide behind objects, the simulacrum for my spirit and mind.

When the happening was over, Jean-Jacques invited me to the after-party but I felt so full of adrenaline from the wildness of the event that I needed to calm down. I never did go to any of the parties that I heard were orgies of sexual liberation. I knew I would have been more exploited than liberated. I couldn't see how this happening, a macho spree of political erotica and sexist turbulence, commemorated our friend Nina. Nonetheless, my participation meant that I was no longer incognito in Paris. I was often greeted by people I didn't know as I walked in Saint-Germain, or in the Coupole, or the Deux Magots.

Both *Pour Conjurer L'Esprit du Catastrophe* and my exhibition at La Librairie Anglaise took place in the autumn of 1963. *Olympia* magazine was interested in doing a feature article on me for their next issue, and Pablo Volta, who had photographed Jean-Jacques's happening, had been commissioned to photograph me. The slant of the article was 'A Day in the Life of an American Artist in Paris'. We visited the Bourget Space Show, where he photographed me standing next to an anti-aircraft missile launcher, gazing at the smooth nose cone of a rocket.

My friend Anne Zamire knew my work and had a wonderful feel for atmospheric places and materials. She took us to an extraordinary, magical, early nineteenth-century café in the Marais. The interior was lined with bevel-edged mirrors that refracted light. It was like a labyrinth of reflections. Pablo's photographs showed an unusual insight into the directions my work would develop. In one shot my profile is eerily reflected in a mirror, part consumed by light; in another I gaze intently at the motion of two white balls on a billiard table. Three years later I created *Liquid Reflections*, in which two clear balls move across a transparent, water-filled disc.

Anne was an actress with the intense gaze of a sorceress, her beautiful face enclosed in a cloud of dark frizzy hair. She was smaller than me and wore layers of dark clothes that she probably picked up at the flea market, where she had her own stall. She was married to a thin, fiercely intelligent man I first met at the Venice Biennale, where he showed me a number tattooed on his arm, his souvenir from Auschwitz. They lived with her father, a painter of Jewish scenes, in a dark apartment in the Marais that reeked of painful memories. I felt very close to Anne. She was Jewish Paris, that part of the cultural world that remained connected to their roots and to their recent memories of persecution and anti-Semitism. She was interested in Jewish mysticism, the Kabbalah, and, like me, in science as well as art.

The Galerie de la Librairie Anglaise was a small subterranean space with low, arched ceilings and white-painted brick walls. This was where my exhibition *Echo-Lights and Vibrographes* would be held. Edwina had promised to pay for an invitation card that I needed to design. The gallery already had a landscape format for their cards, long and quite thin, opening into a double-sided card with enough space for a short text. Michel Courtois wrote the text, 'Mode d'Emploie pour la Vision', in which he says that in my works 'light has returned to its source'.

I decided to print a double exposure, using one of Pablo's photographs of me, Madonna-like, by the rocket nose cone, with the enlarged text of a *Poem Machine*. I persuaded Jean-Loup Charmet to photograph the works I would be exhibiting. We processed the images for the card in his darkroom and, although I had never found him in the least bit attractive, working with him side by side in the dark, with the magic of images surfacing in the developing liquid, created an electric pull between us, leading to us spending what was left of the night together in my bed. Jean-Loup took many photos of me and often followed Nazli and me as I shopped for materials.

The opening was very crowded, and I remember almost nothing but the excitement, and that two *Echo-Lights* were sold. There were reviews: in *Arts*, the critic was not convinced by my *Mille épingles de Lumière* ('A thousand needles of light'); in *Combat*, the surrealist writer José Pierre waxed lyrical, writing that 'Le pinceau tournoyant du phare caresse la trace des larmes sur une joue très pure' ('The returning beam of light caresses traces of tears on a very pure cheek'); and in the *International Herald Tribune*, poet John Ashbery wrote that, although one could not read the text of the *Poem Machines*, perhaps they affected you subliminally.

Many artists came and left their comments. One day Gaïte told me that I had just missed William Burroughs, who particularly liked the show and had told her to ask me to visit him at the Beat Hotel. I noted that Brion Gysin had an exhibition of large calligraphic paintings just opposite La Librairie Anglaise, in the much larger Galerie Stadler. I also noticed that some canvases had Burroughs's text scrawled across them. In the window of La Librairie Anglaise, I had placed a large *Poem Machine* with the text, 'GET RID OF GOVERNMENT TIME TRUE MEN LASER MINDS'. I felt there was a common thread between Brion's work and mine, but I couldn't help but reflect that in Gaïte's tiny gallery two women were expressing very directly powerful revolutionary thoughts, while in a grander, more important gallery, a collaboration between men spoke only indirectly.

The next day, I visited Burroughs in his bare room at the Beat Hotel. He seemed to be expecting me and told me almost immediately how much he liked my works, especially the *Poem Machines*, adding that he wanted his words to move off the page. 'Writing isn't enough,' he drawled in his slow, thoughtful way. He wanted his words to come alive. That was why Brion had written William's text across his canvases, and why they both made recordings and films. He liked my *Vibrograph*. Had I come across Tibetan prayer wheels? I hadn't. He mentioned reincarnation and suggested that perhaps I had been a Tibetan in an earlier life. Nazli could be a reincarnation, he added. Takis had told me that Burroughs liked Nazli. We went out for a coffee, and he asked me if I took drugs. Only a little pot, I replied. 'Well, keep away from hard drugs,' he said. 'I tell all young people that.'

When I told Takis that Burroughs wanted me to put his words on a *Poem Machine*, he looked annoyed. 'Brion would never let him. They don't like women. You don't want to mix your work with theirs.'

During the period of my exhibition, the Italian curator, poet and publisher Arturo Schwarz launched a boxed edition of Man Ray's works in La Librairie Anglaise. That event was my second opening since everyone who came also descended to the basement gallery. Even Man Ray himself found a moment to drop in, accompanied by

Arturo Schwarz, and I was thrilled to meet him and his beautiful wife, Juliet, who graciously invited me to visit them. At the time, he was mainly known for his surrealist photographs and experimental *Rayogrammes*, and his work as a painter was not widely acknowledged. When I visited their home, where he also had his studio, he began to show me his paintings. Man Ray was very intense and, from the way he spoke about his paintings, I realized they were very important to him. Pointing to a platform that served as a storage area for many of his paintings, he asked whether I would like him to bring some down to show me. Not wishing to put him to the trouble of climbing up there, I told him that I was happy enough looking at all the many works hung on the walls. He and Juliet were both warm and friendly, but I didn't see them again for many years.

My exhibition was a coming of age, a graduation from my early 'student' phase into the active world of art. Other artists, poets, critics and even gallerists began to see me as an individual, an artist separate from Takis, with my own voice. I received many invitations to participate in group exhibitions in different galleries in Paris. The Galerie H. Legendre invited me to contribute to a show of artists' boxes, *La Boîte et Son Contenu*. The Galerie Ursula Girardon invited me to participate in the exhibition *Autour du Jeu*. Even Iris Clert finally decided to invite me to show in her *Salon d'Avril 'Les 2004'*.

This was also the winter when Takis and I began to have separate lives. Takis had an older girlfriend, a wealthy society woman with a house of her own near the Luxembourg Gardens. He told me that she bought his clothes and looked after him, which I would never do. I knew that I couldn't behave as she did, but I felt painfully jealous. This reached breaking point the day Takis invited me to a party at her house and I naively accepted. I arrived alone to find the long, narrow room crowded with friends and artists, among whom I particularly remember Alain Jouffroy. The lighting was subdued. Everyone was sitting on couches or chairs placed along the walls, with the door to the room at one end, while the other end was covered by a heavy velvet curtain. Pot was being passed around and, as soon as I entered, I felt a tension in the room. I should have followed my uneasy feeling and left, but pride forced me to stay, and I sat down next to Alain. I wondered why Takis wasn't there; his conspicuous absence was odd. Someone said he had left. I began to wonder what I was doing there. Then, the curtain was drawn and Takis was slowly revealed, stretched out on a bed, cigarette drooping from his mouth, weakly calling, 'Michelle, bring me a glass of water.'

The room went quiet. Heads turned in my direction and, putting on an appearance of total indifference, I stayed for as long as I could bear, then left. As I stood to go, Alain whispered, 'Liliane, you have a great spirit.'

I remembered Takis's words: 'Great spirits don't feel jealousy, they don't need to be attached to anyone, they shine like the sun.'

Once back at La Louisiane, I allowed myself to feel the full extent of the pain and humiliation his betrayal had caused. When I later confronted him, Takis told me he had had a terrible headache and was forced to lie down in the dark. To make matters worse, his lover, Michelle, had bought an *Echo-Light* from my show.

In December, Takis gave me a lovely opal ring for my birthday, telling me that it reminded him of me, iridescent, subtle, full of colour and light. He wanted to make up for the cruel way he had treated me, and he praised me for being such a pure, independent spirit. Like Jean-Paul Sartre and Simone de Beauvoir, we loved each other but had chosen to live in freedom.

Soon after, the gallerist Robert Lewin, who owned the Brook Street Gallery, contacted me from London, and I met him for coffee at the Café de Flore. Although Robert specialized in artists such as Arp, Calder and Morandi, he was also interested in contemporary art and encouraged young gallerists. He liked what the recently opened Signals Gallery was trying to do, namely, to present artists working in new media. Paul Keeler, who with David Medalla had started Signals Gallery, had asked Robert if, while he was in Paris, he might meet me and ask if I would write a text for their new magazine, the first issue of which would be on Takis. They also wanted a statement about my work. Lewin was very straight, serious and a little awkward with me. It was the first time I wrote about my work for a publication.

I decided to cut up the paragraph I wrote, describing my work and intentions, with one taken from a *Scientific American* article about the optics of light.

*

My notebooks at this time were full of sketches of monsters and towers, interspersed with practical notes and texts and sketches for my *Poem Machines*. On the last page of one is a short poem.

> I once lived in a land of pricks
> A strange mountainous land full of sticks
> One dark night I met the King
> Who in joy offered me an opal ring.

For a month or two I lived in a cloud of depression. I had a lover, a Danish artist called Nikolas, who smoked too much pot and drew comic characters in my notebooks. He appeared out of nowhere, in a haze of smoke, one evening with Nazli. He was the silent type and probably needed a place to live. I never knew. I found him attractive, two depressed beings sticking to each other. We slept very late, got out of bed in the afternoon to go and eat, then back to my room at the Hôtel La Louisiane. Takis had left for Greece in February '64 and I had moved into his large corner room. It had a bathroom big enough for me to install a Bunsen burner on a table, on which I stir-fried meals. Nikolas and I would draw, write and generally mess around, until we felt like going to the cinema. Then back to make love, smoke and make more love until stars filled the room. I stagnated and felt time slipping away but I couldn't rouse myself.

And then, it was over. I felt bored with sweet Nikolas, and perhaps he with me. Tearfully, he left for Denmark, and I never saw him again.

Soon after Nikolas left Paris, Takis returned and was not at all happy when I told him about my young lover. After all his lecturing on being free spirits, when it came to my freedom it was hard for him to swallow.

Hôtel La Louisiane was home for several American jazz musicians. The great pianist Bud Powell lived there with his partner, Buttercup. I met Bud in a cheap restaurant, where we habitually went out for dinner, sitting at long benches. He was a large man, sitting alone on the bench across the room, and I heard him ask the waitress for 'a patty'. She couldn't understand and he kept repeating the word louder and louder. It suddenly struck me that he wanted a paté, and I told the waitress. I was immediately rewarded with his big smile. Sometime later, Buttercup came to my room in tears and told me that

Bud was in hospital. They wouldn't let her visit him because she wasn't his legal wife. We have two children, she moaned, and I don't have any money. I lent Buttercup a small amount, and a few days later, she knocked on the door of my room and told me that she still hadn't received the money she'd been waiting for but could repay me in kind. She handed me a small packet that, on opening, revealed an oily black lump, no bigger than the tip of my little finger. 'It's opium, you put a very small amount under your tongue and let it dissolve. It's bitter as hell but it will relieve all kinds of pain. Use it carefully.' She gave me a hug. Buttercup was large. I felt totally embraced by her.

My mind buzzed with ideas for new work. My narrow black notebook *Notes on Radiation Paintings and Vibrations* overflowed with alternative ways to make the luminous spectrum visible or to imagine photons of light, making them move, wiggle, flash, vibrate. There are sketches for cylinders and drums with words or lines, preceding the *Vibrograph* and the *Poem Machines*. I also drew and wrote of making

two cylinders, one inside the other, covered with cheesecloth or another material which,

when turning, make fantastic designs, especially if I dye them varying colours.

This idea came to fruition a year later when I found cylindrical oil filters in Athens, covered with layers of metal mesh that, on spinning, resulted in moiré patterns. Another outcome of this early sketched idea were the kinetic dresses that I made in Paris in late 1966, just before coming to London.

Takis had a close relationship with his dealer Alexander Iolas. When not discussing art or Greek politics, he advised Iolas on his turbulent love life. Some of Iolas's lovers were rough trade and one had cheated on him indiscreetly, robbed and insulted him. Iolas decided to do away with 'the devil'. Takis had to convince him that taking out a hit would end in disaster.

One afternoon, Iolas invited us to his Paris apartment to meet a woman who was bringing him Sarah Bernhardt's Egyptian jewellery. He wanted us to examine it with him to make sure that they weren't fakes. We were excited to see these pieces of ancient art that we'd only seen behind museum glass or in books. Iolas adored Sarah Bernhardt and spoke about her with great passion. Possessing her jewellery would be a deep and fulfilling identification with his idol. The dealer arrived with a large bag and laid out the magnificent pieces, claiming to have authenticating papers. We silently examined them. Iolas then excused himself and took us to another room.

'What did you think? Could they be authentic?'

We knew nothing for certain – after all, we were not experts. We agreed that they looked authentic and were very beautiful.

Iolas walked back, his imperious posture signalling displeasure. We trailed behind him silently.

'I am sorry,' he said, holding up one piece after another and then dropping them on to the table as if they were used rags. 'I cannot believe these really belonged to Sarah Bernhardt. They may well be fake.'

Strong protests from the small, modestly dressed lady who did not look like a swindler.

'Well, perhaps you were cheated.'

More protests.

'Ma chère, they look like second-rate pieces robbed from some inferior tombs.'

'But I have documents.'

'How much do you want for them?'

She named a price.

'Never! These are not worth even a third of that amount. Please take them away,' Iolas exclaimed and started to repack them, gesturing that she should forget the sale.

The lady was aghast. She could not believe what was happening. I could see her crumpling. She lowered her price. Iolas begged her to forget the possibility of his buying such junk. She could not believe her ears, and I was sure that she would leave. But, instead, her eyes imploring, she lowered her price again, saying that it barely covered her costs. She looked so depressed, I thought she might cry. Iolas appeared to think about it, taking up each piece, and then, as if doing her a favour, agreed to that final amount. The poor lady left with her now empty bag. For a moment, Iolas was very still. Then he jumped with joy.

'You believed me, didn't you? You both thought I was doing her a favour to take these items off her hands. But no! They are fantastic, original. I knew it the moment I saw them. Sarah Bernhardt wore them on stage and now they are mine and I got them for nothing. Nothing!!'

*

Hôtel La Louisiane had long been a hub of Saint-Germain-des-Prés intellectual life. Jean-Paul Sartre and Simone de Beauvoir had enjoyed a similar living arrangement there. I stayed, on and off, for two years, much of the time in the room Simone de Beauvoir herself had occupied. One morning, I intended to go to La Bastille to buy some second-hand lenses for my experiments with light. I told Takis, who began to shout that I was too greedy, too ambitious. He accused me of trying to develop my work too fast. In his opinion, I didn't need to buy these lenses. He lectured me on my inflated ego until I left his room, deflated and miserable. Just as I was about to walk through the hotel door in a haze, Sinclair appeared with an American poet he had found somewhere, picked up and given a home. I don't remember her name, but she had an extraordinary gentleness and calm about her. My spirit had been stepped on but, nevertheless, I remained determined and, accompanied by Sinclair's new-found friend, I headed towards boulevard Beaumarchais. It was a clear day, sunshine splashing colours everywhere, but I felt drab and colourless, as if in a grey world. Quite suddenly, I was mesmerized by a pure blue brilliance that made me stop and cry out. My companion was startled. As I moved, the light became green and then yellow, orange, red. My mood changed instantly. The burden of guilt and repressed anger evaporated in this gift of light. I crossed the boulevard to see from what or where it originated. In the window of the second-hand optical store, beside model locomotives and loose camera lenses, were trays of optical glass prisms of varied shapes and sizes. The source of my illumination.

On Building a House and Becoming a Hermit

I arrived in Athens from Geneva, where I had spent a week with Thanos, who was still living with my father and his nanny, Luisa. Thanos was becoming a big, beautiful boy. I loved seeing him grow and took many photos, as if they might replace his everyday presence. Takis had promised that once we built a house in Greece, he would leave Paris for good to live with us both. However, our relationship had been more and more one of two individuals going their own way. We had intense moments of love and harmony, but they were always short. I wanted desperately to make a life together and I continued to believe in Takis's fantasy.

We spent most of the summer living in his sister Tita's apartment in the sweltering city. The badly built block, like so many in central Athens, had large windows, no air conditioning or heating, and thin walls. Cold in winter, simmering in summer. The occupants lived in the shadows, since only at night could they open the shutters and windows to catch the slight breeze that might enter with the mosquitoes and the endless clamour of the city.

Tita's husband, Thanasis Calogeresis, had helped us get clear title to a piece of land by persuading innumerable cousins to agree to the sale – which was why this unassuming man was Onassis's lawyer. We slept very little and spent hours waiting to see officials for permits to build and requests for electricity. We waited our turn, crowded together with men and women carrying live chickens and baskets of produce. We smoothed our way using an introduction from Takis's important architect friend.

Takis's brother Giorgos had a heating company, so we thought he'd be the best person to sort out the heating for Gero Vouno, that bald hill called 'Old Mountain'. Mornings went by sitting in his dusty office, drinking endless cups of Turkish coffee and discussing the merits of different schemes that were never implemented.

On my arrival, Takis took me immediately to

see the land. He'd had the hill dynamited so that we could build the house into it. The back was to protrude just enough for small windows, like windows we'd seen in Pompeii. Designed with slits on the inside that slanted into larger openings on the outer wall, they kept the rooms shady while allowing air to circulate.

Takis had employed a friend of a friend as builder, who had absconded with the advance Takis had mistakenly given him. He left behind a single labourer, Iannis, who was unsuccessfully pickaxing away at the rocky ground.

'Gero Vouno is all rock,' Takis said, taking hold of Iannis's pickaxe. 'The way you are going at it will take a hundred years to cut down this floor. Look, this is how you break it. Keep hitting the same spot until it breaks. You can break anything like that.'

I returned to Paris with Takis at the end of August and spent some more time in Geneva, preparing myself and Thanos, now a chunky, diffident two-year old, for a definitive move to Greece in late autumn. I bought sheets, towels and soft blankets, anticipating our move into the new house. And a German shepherd puppy I named Nango, in memory of the dog that had protected my mother as a child in anti-Semitic Poland.

I was unhappy to leave Paris, where I had developed friendships with other artists, just when gallerists had begun to ask for my work. I realized that I would be isolating myself, but I also thought that I was leaving the world of ambition and commerce to deepen and purify my spirit. And, in Greece, I would finally be with my son.

During the first month, we stayed in Athens with Takis's sister Titika and her three children, leaving Nango with Takis's mother. Takis said Titika was the kindest of his siblings. She'd married a judge, a compassionate and honest man, who was given a job in a remote mountain village that less modest men would have refused. Before he was fifty, he had a heart attack as he was boarding a bus for Athens and died, leaving Titika with three young children and his government pension. Takis helped her eldest son, Nikos, to study architecture at the Beaux Arts in Paris. In exchange, Nikos, a quiet, plodding young man, drew up all his uncle's sculptures. Titika lived in a modern apartment building just off Patisseon Street. The apartment wasn't large, but she gave me my own room, which I shared with Thanos.

Thanos had been very excited to come with me to Greece, but in Athens he became fearful and disturbed and began to wet his bed every night. I didn't know what to do and relied on Titika for advice. Thanos accompanied me during the day, sitting upright in the front of the car, quiet, uncomplaining, good as gold, waiting endlessly as I negotiated with builders. But at night, after I told him a story and put him in his crib, he cried and slept fitfully. Being a mother was a new experience for me. It didn't occur to me that his careful behaviour during the day was his way of telling me that he was no trouble and that I should not abandon him in this place of strange, incomprehensible voices. At night, everything fell apart.

When I had a difficult day, I would take him to Terma Patissia and leave him in the care of Krystallo and Takis's mother, who both welcomed him with such fervour that, if it hadn't been for the presence of Nango, who was also there, and their goat and cackling chickens, Thanos would not have stayed.

Takis was in Paris, busy making work to sell to

Iolas, so we would have enough money to continue. The land had been bought with money I had saved while living in New York. My father sent me an allowance at irregular intervals, which in New York I collected from the Fifth Avenue office of his business colleague Joe Axler. One day Joe had a surprise for me: 'You're a lucky girl. Your crazy father has sent you five grand. Don't spend it all at once.' I put it in the bank and hardly touched it, so when we needed money to buy Gero Vouno, I had it ready. My father subsequently helped us meet many of the building bills. He was so proud that I'd not frittered away my allowance that he kept bragging about it to all his friends. He didn't save at all, didn't even invest his earnings when his business did well. He simply spent more, saying, 'I want to live like a lion and die like a mouse.' Everyone thought he was a millionaire, but whatever he made burned through his pockets. He didn't believe in ownership and, apart from clothes and personal belongings, his only investment was in mobility. He owned a cream Chrysler convertible with red leather seats, rare in Europe in the early 1960s. Even when he had the capital to invest in an apartment, he preferred to rent. He believed 'money should flow', but also told me that many Jews had died in concentration camps because they had not wanted to abandon their properties.

I was so busy working on the house that I didn't have much time to shop for food or even think about my own work. Titika, her awkward but lovely teenage daughter, Maria, and her youngest son, Dani, whom she spoiled, were all very kind to me and Thanos, feeding and looking after us. Food is an important part of Greek hospitality, and its purchase and preparation dominated the evening's conversation. I was interested because it was all new to me, as was the language that I was quickly learning. The only person in Takis's large family who spoke English was Tita. I knew that I had to speak and understand Greek, because we did not have an architect. We had hired craftsmen to do separate jobs and I had to make sure they did what they were supposed to do and did it well.

During the spring and summer of 1964, once the hill was dynamited and the foundation laid, the outer walls were raised and the concrete roof poured. Iron rods protruded from the top, bent at different angles like ungainly dancing figures. We left them to build a second floor that would be our astronomical centre, and I made sketches for it in my notebooks. On one visit to the building site I noticed a concrete appendage sticking out halfway along the east side of the beautifully curved structure. It was mostly underground with narrow, horizontal, slatted windows facing south.

'Kitchen and bathroom,' Takis announced.

It was much too small and ugly.

'Why would we need a large kitchen?' he said rhetorically, since it was a fait accompli.

And who would spend time in that narrow, pokey room? Me, since Takis didn't cook.

We had our first quarrel about the house. The first of many disagreements that I was to learn were quite normal when building, since each person builds a nest according to their own needs and visualization of space and its functionality.

The house was built into the hill and sheltered by the land at the back and on part of the west side. The windows were mainly on the east side, allowing the morning sun to illuminate the large space. While Takis was still in Greece, we agreed to leave the openings larger towards the front, which faced south, with floor-to-ceiling glass doors leading to a large marble terrace. It would be up to me to decide how to make these large windows, what material to use and to find the appropriate craftsmen.

Many old buildings in Athens were being pulled down and replaced by apartment blocks. The old romantic villas had large marble balconies and marble slabs for floors. Athenians who did keep their old villas often exchanged the marble slabs for fashionable *mosaici* — small pieces of different-coloured marble cemented together in smart designs or thrown together randomly, and then polished. Their loss was our gain. We bought large marble slabs at bargain prices. Our mason, a formidably built man, used a technique for moving the marble that was as old as the Parthenon. He rolled the slabs on top of wooden poles and carefully levered them up, helped by one of his burly men. These slabs were destined for the floor, which Iannis had so painfully prepared. We used the balconies and their spiral supports as benches inside and out.

Our initial idea was to keep the ground floor open plan but, because the rocky ground was so difficult to level, we decided to leave the back a few steps higher, turning defeat to our advantage. Before Takis left, we shaped the ground where the floor level changed into a pleasing curve and laid the floor slabs. We liked the feel of the open space, but the change in floor level suggested that the back of the house would be just right for bedrooms. We decided that they would feel more protected if we separated them with walls. We drew chalk lines on the floor where we wanted the walls built for three bedrooms and a dining room opposite the galley kitchen. In the middle of the curved stepped area, we decided to leave a semi-circular space for a library, from where the second bedroom would be entered. We disagreed when it came to the dining area. Takis wanted to enclose it with a wall, saying that it would be more symmetrical seen from the front, a straight wall, then a curved space and then another straight wall. I agreed it would look nice from the outside, but that it would be cramped and dark on the inside since, unlike the bedrooms, it wouldn't even have a small window. I argued that we should build a waist-high wall to separate it from the front area and the hallway that led to the kitchenette, bathroom and third bedroom. Since that was also cheaper to build, he finally agreed, probably realizing that I was right.

Takis had been advised to lay a damp course at the back of the house, where the rooms were almost entirely underground, but he insisted that the house was built on dry rock, and we did not need one. He was, unfortunately, proven wrong when, after the first rains, the back walls were visibly damp. The rain, it seemed, had seeped through the porous rock. We solved what had appeared quite a disaster by cutting drainage gulleys along the back and side walls to guide rainwater away from the building.

Driving back from seeing Takis off at the airport, I stopped at a small playground in Phaliron to let Thanos play. It was a bright, wintry day, and the playground was almost empty, the few children muffled in their coats and scarves. I sat and watched a plane overhead, thinking sadly, there he goes and here am I, misplaced and unsure of where I'm heading. I felt that my life was interrupted once again, the daily rhythm that I had gradually acquired while working in Paris now replaced with a new way of life. On the one hand, I was excited to take on the responsibility of building the house on Gero Vouno, but on the other, the adventure was sure to be chaotic, anxious, exhausting, experienced from moment to moment, at times pleasurable and at others miserable and lonely. I had also decided to be with my child, thinking that Takis's family would support me, but not realizing just how disorientated and frightened he would feel, dropped suddenly into an unfamiliar world. Thinking of doing something is so different from living the experience.

Having told me which were the nicest cafés in Athens, Takis warned me to stay away from the Athenian art world. Nothing good would come of that, he told me, and, being naive and still somehow pinned fast under his thumb, I listened. Apart from Minos and Amy, who were now living in Athens, I hardly met any Greek artists or poets. In fact, during my first winter in Athens, I lived like a hermit, seeing only builders, craftsmen and Takis's family.

It was a time of introspection. I began to read the life of Rechnung Milarepa.

Takis liked to use Nazli as an example of a pure woman without ego or morals. I thought it more likely that she had been abused so often, she had become detached from her own feelings. In Paris, about a year earlier, to make more money she had started selling heroin and someone had grassed on her. In trouble, she left for Morocco but didn't have enough money to buy train tickets. She chose to hitchhike and found herself walking at night with her six-year-old son, Juba, across the Pyrenees. Somehow, she managed to get to Tafraout. There, she soon ran out of money but, she told me, the Moroccan men were all interested in fucking her and gladly paid her for the privilege. She didn't seem to mind at all and said that they were all so nice and it was an easy life and so beautiful, until the police found out, forcing her to leave town. She laughed as she recounted her misadventures. I felt a great friendship for Nazli.

Some weeks before I left Paris, Nazli had travelled to London in great excitement, because John Calder had promised to publish her poems in a new anthology of young British poets.* She was expecting a large advance and had decided to leave for India immediately afterwards, with Juba. Predictably, Calder was not as forthcoming as she'd hoped, and she left for India with a one-way ticket and a hundred pounds. Nevertheless, she bought a precious gift for Takis, three volumes of the life and songs of Tibet's greatest poet saint, Milarepa. Once in India, Nazli hoped to make a film of Milarepa's life. Although the leather-bound books were meant

* 'New Writers' series, 1965–7, Calder & Boyars.

for Takis, he expressed little interest, so I took them with me to Athens.

I became obsessed with Milarepa, reading all three volumes over and over, until I knew them almost by heart. I began to identify with him. I sought to purify myself; to divest myself of ego, as if it were a filthy suit of clothing that I could rip off and cast away. I wanted to feel like the wind and the sky. My sincere intentions were to keep silent and watch my behaviour; to rid myself of all negative emotions. The house on Gero Vouno would be my cave on a hill. Looking back through my painful diaries, I now see that the house I was building on the bare dusty hill in Attica was my inner house, the structure of my spirit and my psyche.

I found a small apartment with a sunny terrace near Titika's building, where Thanos and I lived for the whole of the winter and the spring of 1965, impatiently waiting to move to Gero Vouno. I hired a young Greek girl to help look after Thanos and our apartment, while I supervised the building works and rushed around buying materials and getting permits.

I was in the apartment when I had my first experience of an earthquake. I was feeding Thanos, enduring the usual battle to convince him to eat the food I had so carefully prepared, when his dish started sliding on the shuddering table. We were on quite a high floor, and I hoped the building would not collapse. Thanos began to cry. The whole room seemed to tilt. Dropping the spoon, I pulled him from his highchair and held him close. Not knowing if I should run down the stairs, I froze until it stopped.

A few days later, I had a visitor from New York. Takis had called, asking me to look after this friend of one of his collectors. I spent the two days he was in Athens showing him around all the important cultural sites, while he regaled me with stories of his life. Arthur King was a famous jeweller and a personal friend of Jackie Kennedy, for whom he'd made a pink diamond ring, changing the colour by altering its atomic structure. He spoke continuously, with such great energy that I felt exhausted at the end of each day. He was gay and Jewish but had converted to Catholicism. Everything Arthur had, made or did, had to be the best, the finest. He was admirable, but exactly what I went to Greece to escape: the tight world of ambition, in which nothing is ever good enough, and no one stops long enough to enjoy what is there.

New York, Paris, Geneva: in all these cities, in different ways, I felt the sickening richness of materiality and the 'have to have it', the need to be at the top or at least immersed in a gaudy, turbulent current. In Athens, everything slowed down; enveloped in fine dust and sunlight, I had the time to smell the world and partake of its unadorned treasures. I would visit the empty Acropolis and the museum to meditate on the culture that had had an understanding of space now lost to us. On leaving, Arthur gave me a pink pearl twisted into the shape of a cross. I thanked him profusely but wondered whether it had been bombarded by electrons to become a Christian pearl.

I walked around Athens, looking at doors and windows, trying to decide what material to use and how to design them. I soon realized that wood was out of the question. It was expensive in Greece, and we'd have problems with maintenance. Aluminium seemed to be the best material to use because of its lightness and weathering capacity, but Greece was not yet industrialized, and it was difficult to find companies who made aluminium windows and door frames. The ones I did find were hugely expensive, and probably imported, so I decided to have the frames made from mild steel and painted.

Looking for a blacksmith to do the job, I came across a smithy owned by a young man in his early twenties. Sakis was very hardworking and looked older than his age, his face leathery and taut. He became our blacksmith and my friend, if I could say that of an uneducated man with whom I had very little in common. Takis had said, 'Be careful with men, here in Greece. They are not like men in Paris or New York. They are peasants, and any involvement can lead to tragedy.'

Supervising the work, I spent a lot of time in the smithy, getting to know Sakis. He often took me up to Gero Vouno on the back of his motorcycle and, holding on to him, I felt attracted. I was curious about how he became the owner of the workshop, and he told me his story. At thirteen, he had left home to find work, and walked to Athens from his village in the mountains of the Peloponnese. He found a blacksmith who was willing to take him on as an apprentice. They didn't pay him but allowed him to sleep on the floor of the shop and gave him scraps to eat. His first winter, he was so hungry that he scavenged in the fields and ate raw artichokes. Slowly, he began to learn the trade, and whenever he made a bit of money, he would buy himself tools, until he had enough to begin work on his own. When he finally set up his own shop, he hired young men and treated them well. I admired Sakis for his courage, and the intelligence that had allowed him to survive and thrive. When I enthused about astronomy, he seemed not to know that the Earth was a planet that revolved around the sun. I tried to explain the solar system and he looked at me steadily and then said, 'But you are my cosmos.' I realized that perhaps we had become too close, and when he invited me to go to a film, I declined and then felt dreadful about letting him down. I could see that he took my refusal as a message that he wasn't good enough for someone like me, that he was hurt and insulted, which reminded me of Takis's admonishments.

I was at the house every day, often with but at times without little Thanos, who was now acclimatized to the exaggerated attentions of his Greek family.

Our land lay at the top of the ancient hill. Mount Parnis rose to the north of it, while, in between Gero Vouno and Parnis, a green valley was cultivated by farmers from Menidi.

Just behind the building works on the hill, wild thyme and sage bushes perfumed the air. I often took peaceful walks there with Nango, feeling a great sense of freedom. I continually thought about the works I would develop. Unfortunately, Plexiglass was very expensive in Athens so, to begin realizing my new ideas, I decided to sand and polish the many works I had brought from New York. These were the ones I had made by extruding plastic into fine lines and heating it to become one with the clear acrylic sheet or the later polymer reflection 'paintings'. I took some to Sakis's workshop, where he allowed me to use his electric hand tools to sand down the surfaces. But they were stubborn and didn't polish up as I had hoped. Obstinately working on them, I realized that to take energy from an object or an action, one needed to exhaust one's feeling, whether it was fatigue, hunger, cold, anger, jealousy or passion – each had to be experienced completely.

I couldn't understand why I felt so sleepy, so much so that I would doze off while leaning against a wall in the sun. I thought it was my bad karma and wished I could sleep less. I wanted to be awake and alert all the time. Overseeing builders and craftsmen was not only difficult but also enervating, since I became irritated by their sloppiness, by the inevitable breakages and mistakes they made. I had no experience in dealing with several people at a time, or even one, for that matter. The learning curve was steep, and all in Greek, but I took that for granted, which was probably thanks to my experience in Lugano, where I had been dropped into a school where no one spoke English and I had to learn Italian on the fly, while absorbing the lessons. Learning the language was just something one did in another country. My builders certainly spoke no other tongue. Later, Greek friends in Athens would say, 'Liliane speaks builders' Greek.'

Takis's light-haired, delicate brother Giorgos, who was supposed to install our heating, came to take measurements, and pronounced, 'How can you live up here? This is a monastery.' I wanted to live as an ascetic in a bare, silent place. I didn't like the sound of my voice, feeling I spoke mechanically. I wanted to walk to the sound of the Japanese shaku-hachi flute, played by wandering Zen monks wearing baskets over their heads.

In the middle of February, I decided to go to Paris, since Takis would not be coming to Greece for a while. I made a small cylinder for him 'as the round sun-like poem cylinder of the MIND. An offering to him and the Buddhas, to Milarepa to please help me conquer jealousy and my own Ego extinguish'. It seemed from my diaries that Takis had become my guru. But I was a rebellious disciple with a strong will and, no matter how hard I tried and how many vows I made, I could not dominate my ego.

Sakis helped me make the small *Poem Machine*, using a metal oil filter that I found in a car-part shop in Athens. I wrote the poem and called it 'Man is Naked'. Whereas all my earlier, much larger *Poem Machines* had rotated at quite high speeds, this one turned more slowly, allowing one to almost read the poem. The fact that I couldn't follow the words sequentially, although I could clearly see them, was a new and interesting development that I called 'chaotic'.

An Interlude in Paris

FEBRUARY 1965

To be back in Paris was like a shot of adrenaline. I was no longer used to the pace of everyday life with Takis, but I felt liberated from the responsibilities of building, of looking after a small child and a dog, allowing me to fully concentrate on my work.

Paul Keeler had come from London with his collaborators, David Medalla and Guy Brett, to speak to us about their new gallery named after Takis's iconic work *Signals*. It was on four floors in a building on the corner of Welbeck and Wigmore Streets that was part of the Keeler ophthalmic empire. David and Paul were planning to exhibit art inspired by science and by artists from different parts of the planet. They were all about my age: Guy refined and physically attractive; David elfin and brilliant; Paul enthusiastic, practical and financially able to make it happen. Paul waxed lyrical about my new *Poem Machine* and asked me to consign it to the gallery, offering me a show in November 1965.

I spent ten days in Paris and returned energized to Athens. I immediately started making new conical works, which I later called *Poemcons*. I found a wood turner in Athens to make these to my sketched proportions and began thinking of texts I could use and the way I wanted them to look. One idea I had was to use very thin fonts in large sizes that would look more like hieroglyphs when seen in motion. The first one I made came out a mess, and I decided I would plan each one precisely. I overpainted the messy one and relettered it, allowing the earlier letters to partially show through. As fate would have it, that one, *Atom Body Was Light*, was the only one to survive Takis's critique.

Things were difficult with the building work. We were short of money, and I was very concerned not to make mistakes. Takis had made Giorgos responsible for signing the IOUs for all the stage payments, because he was a Greek male and family, but he either forgot or signed them all at once, causing me to worry that we would be ripped off. As both a foreigner and a woman, it was especially difficult for me to supervise the building work and ensure that everything was done well and completed before payment. I had a battle on my hands at every meeting. The men behaved as if they were doing me a favour working for me, but I was paying dearly for those favours.

When I dreamed, it was in Greek. I spoke it all day and my mind churned, wiping out my mother tongue. I could no longer think.

I began to meet people returning from India or going there. One of them showed me a prayer wheel. I was amazed at its lightness and the elegance of its construction. I wanted to make something similar and started sketching what I later called my *Poem Wheels*. Takis, always inconsistent, loved the cones I sent him and wrote that now my works would make people happy.

I have captured a mathematical rhythm.

My moods swung up and down. One minute I was full of self-criticism, the next I felt exhilarated. I was most happy and calm when making art. Why?

Because making art is a meditation – but, I discovered, so was dancing:

> April 13th – Tonight, I went to a taverna and heard Bazouki and also folkdance music. An old bus conductor danced so proudly – stylised, making the night his own.

He was completely absorbed, elegant and gracious. He had slipped beyond his age, his class, to become his dance.

My father visited with his girlfriend and neither liked Gero Vouno, but he left me enough money to finish the building. I no longer had to worry about the unpaid bills and all the things I had to buy to move in.

Thanos turned three on 17 April, growing more independent. Towards the end of April, there were beautiful warm days of sunshine and clear skies. I was up on our hill in the sun, reading and cutting up a poem the American poet George Andrews had given me when I was last in Paris, asking me to put it on a *Poem Machine*. 'Delphic Delirium's nine pages were much too long, but he had permitted me to edit it. I kept intact what he expressed, placing three words in three rows vertically. From nine pages, I condensed it to nine words and called it *Beyond Images*.

As the house neared completion, I found more time to concentrate on my work and made more wood-turned cones, Letrasetting poems on to them. I also had cylinders turned in wood, one in several parts that spun independently. I painted it red and yellow and used numbers, letters and a few simple words as a special *Poem Wheel for Thanos*, to teach him to read and count.

Takis had encouraged me to use my early works to make new material, since it was so difficult to obtain Plexiglass in Athens. You have so much material, he would say. Just clean it and you can make new works. I had gone about it methodically, sanding down each work, obliterating my earlier experiments, only to discover that no matter how hard I tried, I couldn't polish the Plexiglass surfaces. Milarepa told his disciples to polish the mirror of their minds by meditating on the pure blue sky. Realizing that to really cleanse my mind of ignorance and prejudices was so much harder than to polish the surface of my old Perspex works, I despaired of ever being able to reach even the lowest rung of pure mind. I would not give up: I would somehow clean the Perspex, therefore it must also be possible to polish the mirror of my mind. My days were an emotional roller coaster, depression following exhilaration.

Nazli's sister, Laila, came to stay and brought the confusing news that Takis was in Paris, when I'd thought he was in New York. I wondered why he hadn't written to me.

Living in Gero Vouno

It was good to have Laila with me, especially since on 10 May we moved to Gero Vouno, taking everything there in numerous trips. Then began the honeymoon of living there.

I loved its silence and bareness. I even loved not having electricity. Candles or paraffin lamps sputtered and filled the house with their industrial smell. We sat on the marble-slabbed terrace in cheap deckchairs and looked out over Athens to the sea beyond. I did not want to go into Athens, but there were still so many things to do. Living in Gero Vouno gradually changed my life. I began to practise Hatha yoga daily, concentrating on breathing exercises.

But the house was isolated, and I felt vulnerable alone there with a small child. Strangers appeared at the house more often than I had expected. The locals couldn't believe we had built this round, half-underground house as a dwelling. Most thought it was a cinema — so we often had visitors, curious to see what we were doing. Nango was too friendly to these uninvited visitors. I wanted a new dog. I gave Nango to my mother-in-law, who was happy to have him. Laila and I went to Corinth in my Mini Traveller to see a man selling Belgian shepherds. Four dogs were left, larger than I expected at four months old. I chose the only female, sleek and black with bright yellow eyes. I thought she would make a good guard dog. Just seeing her might frighten someone off. He gave me one of his old T-shirts to comfort her for the first days. I thought he was exaggerating, but on the way back to Athens she fretted and clawed the back of the car, terrified to be enclosed in a moving vehicle with two strangers. She kept the T-shirt in her mouth or between her paws for three days and on the fourth she let it fall to the floor and showed no more interest in it. She reminded me of Anubis, so I decided to call her Cleopatra, which became Cleo. She sat at my side, ears pricked up, alert. With anyone unfamiliar, she would stand between us, not allowing them to approach me. Apart from that, she was wild and difficult to control. The breeder had given me the name of a young Scot in Athens, who owned Cleo's father and trained Alsatians. He agreed to take her for a week. She returned much calmer. 'This is only the beginning,' he warned me. 'You need to continue training her to make her your dog.' He showed me how to make her sit and stay, how to get her to heel, or to inspect our boundaries, now fenced with bright blue wire. I had to run out to the gate, making excited sounds. She would run out with me, barking loudly. I would continue running noisily around the perimeter and she would happily join me. I had to do this every time anyone came to the gate, and even if no one came, a few times daily. In less than a week, all I needed to do was make the same sounds, even quietly, and Cleo would bounce up and rush out barking to see who might be approaching.

My father would turn up unexpectedly, perhaps on his way to the Far East on business, to check how I was getting on and to lie basking in the sun for hours, asking me how I could choose to live in a shit-hole country when I had the choice of living in Paris, Geneva or New York. Who would choose to live in a slum? When he left, I would feel sad, sensing his loneliness and his inability to share in my achievements.

Again and again, I ask myself what am I doing, who am I, with intervals, when I take up everyday life; an artist – with developments in my work almost too fast for me to comprehend. I am working with poems – words, thoughts, forms, movement, light. What I want is to give deep meaning to one word, to enrich a poem or a combination of words by mixing in new words, by changing sequence with speed – let the imagination be sparked by word on the wing! Language is the shell to crack to find the fruit of poetry.

Early in June, Takis arrived like a cyclone, sweeping all aside. I was so happy to see him and for a few days we were all harmony, until he settled and found fault with my arrangements and mistakes in the building that irritated him. He couldn't see how much I'd accomplished, allowing him to continue his work in Paris. When I spoke about my own problems, he said I never stopped complaining. I told myself to be still, to enjoy his being here at last. It also looked like Keeler had changed his mind about the autumn exhibition of my work. I was very disappointed.

We hired two girls to look after the house, but I was not good at delegating or teaching them how to keep a household, not really knowing myself. My relationship with Takis was tense. So much expectation had built up, which disintegrated little by little as our egos collided. I tried to adapt, to be more considerate, to expect less from him, but there was no tranquillity. He was bored in Gero Vouno. We spent time with his family, who commented that the building was so strange. They made him nervous, all except his mother. He enjoyed sitting with her in her garden of bare earth and goat droppings, around the uneven table, smoking, joking and teasing. There, he relaxed, at one with himself.

Takis liked to teach, and I was his willing rough diamond to cut, shape and polish until it shimmered and sparkled. When he left for Paris after three tumultuous weeks, I wept and he consoled me, forgetting all his tools.

Early in July, I left for Mykonos with Thanos, Cleo and a girl Tita had found: 'She was herding goats in a mountain village, she will be happy to work just for food and board.' All Tita's servants slept in the hall on some rags on the floor. It seemed normal to them that they should be treated so. I paid the girl and made sure she had her own room.

Every spring the women of Mykonos painted their houses and the streets with whitewash, because it was antiseptic and reflected the light. The house I rented was old, simple and rustic. I loved the smell of thyme and sage that pervaded it. I planned to stay for two weeks but, charmed by the delight of easy living, that stretched to a month. Every morning, after our simple breakfast of rich sheep's yogurt and honey, dry rusks and hot chocolate or coffee, I took Thanos and the girl to the small boat that transported them to the beach. I joined them later, walking there with Cleo along the shoreline, barefoot, with time to think.

It seemed to me that it was very difficult to change one's character, because no matter how often I promised myself I would not talk or I would think carefully before speaking, I still found myself forgetting.

July 5th – I see everything I am doing now is connected to the circle; cylinder, cones, disks, all are circular.

July 9th – Today, as I walked to the beach, I realised that it is very important for me not to talk, to lose the habit of showing off, of wanting people to like and admire me. Deep underneath, when these things have crumbled, when one goes beyond the word, through the quiet of oneself and the control of what one utters, there will come a new richness, an awareness that will bring great joy. Today I practised walking, feeling the earth and cosmos, and I realised that I only have the soles of my feet attached to the earth. The rest of my body is in the air.

Those soles, however, were in contact with the earth. I felt that we neglected them. I sensed their hidden importance. I continued my yoga breathing, breathing in and out and holding the breath each time. I found it interesting that in yoga teaching it is equally important to keep the lungs empty as to hold them full of air. I wondered whether that thought overlapped into behaviour, ethics. To give equal importance to not having as to having. That thought could change society.

On Mykonos, I bumped into Pat Getz, a friend from my schooldays who was visiting her painter mother. She was now an archaeologist and would become a leading expert on Cycladic art. We reminisced about our years in Solebury. I also spotted Mr and Mrs Ritter, my Latin and English literature teachers at Solebury. I greeted them and they marvelled at how I had changed. They seemed the same. They would not have recognized me, but I had a good memory for faces that had impressed me.

Mykonos also brought me together again with Victoria Barr. We spent time on the beach and at a taverna in the evenings, where we sat and watched the local men dance. Offered drinks by two young dancers, we ended up dancing together, connected with high-held handkerchiefs. When we left, they followed us, asking whether we might like to go for a walk on the beach. Victoria and I were used to being approached and knew what a stroll on the beach inevitably led to, but what the hell, we were on holiday, tanned and feeling sexy. My young man, a wonderful dancer, had been asked to dance in a foreign film but earned his living as an electrician. On another evening, he came to my house. The heat was unbearable and drove us up on to the roof where we made love under the stars.

In August, Takis still in Paris, we returned to

Gero Vouno. The fields were a deep ochre and our house, which we'd painted an earth colour, blended into the landscape in just the way we'd hoped it would. The windows' metal frames were light blue to make them seem like part of the sky, and the house, from outside and inside, felt like a natural outcrop of the hill. The earth steamed with heat and fine dust. We still had no electricity, so I bought a large ice box, but the ice delivery man refused to come to the top of the hill. By the time my young girl had fetched a large block of ice up to the house there was never very much left.

My mother came with my brother Dennis, sent by my father to check up on me. They were sweet and we enjoyed our time together. Just before Takis' return to Athens, my mother left, taking Thanos with her. I hoped that being alone with Takis would make it easier, since he was not happy around children, even his own.

During the two months Takis and I spent together we planted a row of cypresses along the boundary and a grove of young olive trees. Takis taught me the essentials of how to work with plaster, a technique he had learned from a wise old Egyptian. I wrote all the steps methodically into my diary and made my first plaster head, following his eight steps, but it came out a little wide and I didn't make a second one. We took an impromptu trip to one of the Cycladic islands, where we passed several strange days. Takis had been told it was easy to find somewhere to rent, but the few houses and rooms were all taken. Someone let us use their tiny shepherd's hut, where we slept on a straw mattress in one small room. I felt happy to bathe in the sea on the deserted beach, but Takis didn't swim and disliked water with the excuse that he was born under the sign of Scorpio.

October 2nd — A few days before Takis left for Paris, he had a dream that was very important. He saw three of his cousins, his aunt Afroditi's children, smeared with red paint, hitting a magnet, which was placed between them. He told me this meant that they were hitting the unknown. They were aggressive to the stranger. These children had been neglected by their parents, their father a drunkard and their mother always away, working as a servant. Takis said that all children who had been neglected grew into aggressive adults. There were differences. If they had been openly neglected, they would feel a deep need for love, and they might behave in such a way as to make people love them. They might become great leaders like Theseus or Romulus, but they could also degenerate into criminals. There were parents who neglected their children but pretended that they didn't. This is perhaps worse because it confuses the child and they do not look elsewhere for love. They believe they are loved but feel they are not. He said this was my problem. I did not understand psychology. He said that I needed to be dominated by other people's lives and their problems to understand them and through them myself. I should forget myself and confuse myself with other people. He said, there should not be a Liliane because in reality there isn't one Liliane. To know myself I needed to know everyone else.

What did I know, at that time, about psychology? At eighteen, I had read Freud's *Totem and Taboo*, and immediately thought of my father. How

I would cringe at him lying stretched out in his underpants, tanned barrel chest bare, basking in the sun, scratching his crotch, gorging on chocolates or cherries. His powerful appetites disturbed me. Perhaps I felt that he might eat me too. I had read *Lolita* and identified with the abused and depressed teenager – repulsion but also, undoubtedly, erotic fascination. Takis was fifteen years older than me, a more romantic father figure. Often, I felt as if I were his little child, whom he reprimanded, instructed and cared for, but also fucked. He was absorbed by ancient Greek or Egyptian knowledge, but I doubted he had read either Freud or Jung. That was not the kind of psychology he was referring to. He knew nothing of transference. Perhaps he unconsciously hoped that by guiding me to shed my ego, to be compassionate, quiet, undemanding, these qualities, so painfully earned by me, would pass to him.

I drew *Poem Wheels*, I wrote poems, I spent hours in machine shops, waiting while the toolmaker finished his serious work, so that he could help me make mine. These shops reeked of the acrid smell of metal; their noise was a grinding and banging. They were small, hot in summer and cold in winter. I wrote many poems for the cylinders, most of which would either not be made or, having been made, would vanish, given away, not then considered by me as of value.

WORLD

WORD

WAR

WIND

WONDER

SALE

SUN

SING

SOAR

A New Freedom

AUTUMN 1965

Towards the end of October, Titika asked me if I would like to hire her friend Ruby, an educated, middle-class woman, divorced and childless. She needed a job and would be happy to work as my housekeeper and nanny. She turned out to be wonderful, teaching Thanos Greek, picking wild herbs in the barren fields around the house for special salads.

One evening, after Thanos had been put to bed and I was sitting reading by the fireplace, she brought out a pack of cards and asked me if I would like her to read them for me. She shuffled the pack, asked me to cut, dealt them out face down then told me to choose some. She looked carefully, then said, 'I see your husband sitting between a woman and a man. He is talking to the woman, but the man looks the other way. They are on an island. She is powerful and may help him, but she will want something in exchange.'

Ruby put these cards to one side and asked me to choose a few more. 'Now, I see you. This is later, sometime in the future, but I see you living on an island. You will be protected by a good man, and you will give birth to another child, a girl.'

I was amazed. I felt the woman was a witch with special powers of foresight. I loved having her with us. I knew she cared for me and felt protected by her. She would tell me, 'You are living here like a nun. You are young. Go enjoy yourself.'

Autumn was full of intoxicating odours as new wine was put into resinated barrels, and everywhere one inhaled the aroma of tree sap, the fragrance of the forest. A small taverna, halfway down the hill, stocked their own retsina, made from white grapes and kokineli, a resinated wine from red grapes. For months, I'd been watching men building their illegal shacks at night on their small parcels below our land. The women watched out for police patrols at dawn. If they spotted one, they beat pans and pots and screamed and wailed if the roof was not yet laid. The police often took fright, or pity on them, and departed in clouds of dust. I loved staying up at night to watch the men's shirtless bodies, gleaming with sweat, in the light of oil lamps and moonshine, dancers moving around their rising structures. I was the hidden spectator as their women and children were too busy carrying bricks or water from the communal tap or bringing food for the men.

In 1965, in Athens, it was extremely difficult for many self-employed to obtain legal permits to drive a small truck or taxi, so *piratis*, pirate taxis, flourished. When I needed to go to Athens, I'd call the same *piratis* to collect me at Gero Vouno and pick me up later, usually in Syntagma Square. Café Papaspirou was on one corner, across the street from American Express. It was the favourite haunt of American and English poets, artists and travellers, some on their way from or to India and Nepal.

I saw *Help!*, the Beatles' film, and was so overwhelmed by the energy of the music and the sense of freedom it unleashed that I couldn't leave until after the last performance. I wondered if I had missed all that, in my ascetic hilltop home. I had spent two years building the house, simultaneously endeavouring to tear down the shanty town of my inner lodgings. Had my constant self-bullying given some fruit? I wasn't sure, but the film had unleashed a feeling inside me of wanting to break loose. After the cinema closed, I walked dreamily to Syntagma Square and bumped into a young man. We greeted each other simultaneously, as if we were old friends. He asked if I would like a coffee.

That was how I met Leonard D. Marshall, a young American poet who used to hang around the Beat Hotel in Paris. He'd skipped bail in Louisiana, where he was up for a bum drug charge, and was on the run. His appearance was so ordinary he reminded me of Burroughs. He read the *Wall Street Journal* and when I asked him why, he said, 'If you can keep track of where the money is going, you know what's happening in the world.' A decidedly interesting point of view. Lennie wrote very short poems that had never been published. His friends knew them by heart, and they circulated orally. I asked him to give me some to use on my *Poemcones*.

On the morning of 11 November, Cleo ran to the gate, barking furiously, and there was Sinclair, laughing sheepishly, teeth black and pointed, eyes hooded, body skeletal.

'Call off Anubis, he wants to kill me! Is your fence electric?'

I opened the gate. 'Cleo won't hurt you, even if you look like a demon from hell.'

'I come from hell,' Sinclair answered in his South African accent. 'I have been to hell and back. I was locked up in a clinic, where they knocked out all my caps. I escaped, and I've come to see Takis.'

'Well, he isn't here.'

'Does that mean I have to leave?' Sinclair was always a bit afraid of Takis and his prohibitions.

I welcomed him in with pleasure and Sinclair recounted his last five years, even though we'd seen each other during that time. He complained that his wealthy mother wouldn't give him any money and kept sending him to the loony bin. But Sinclair was not mad, just a repressed B, according to Takis's categorization. 'When everyone thought I was mad in Paris, I initiated spontaneous theatre, more advanced than happenings,' he said.

He asked if he could stay at Gero Vouno since, as usual, he had no money. I agreed on the condition that he listened to me and behaved himself. He was as submissive as a child and promised to be good.

One frequenter of Papaspirou café was Panos

Koutrouboussis, a Greek poet with an interest in magic and esoteric knowledge. He was slight, with a beautiful face and a sardonic sense of humour. His English was fluent, after a scholarship to the American College in Athens, given because his judge father had been assassinated during the civil war. He was passing around a special book. I opened it on a photograph of the author, Franz Bardon, who looked straight through me. Seeing I was struck, Panos lent it to me. *Initiation into Hermetics* was not a theoretical book. Bardon had written a practical guide to reaching a higher spiritual plane through greater control over one's thoughts and actions. I decided to practise his teaching and began to work systematically on his method for thought control and visualization meditation. He wrote that it was not only important to still the mind and empty it of undirected thoughts, it was also essential to learn to visualize. One experiment he suggested reminded me of a class conducted by Mr Andrews, my tenth-grade teacher at Solebury. He asked us to look carefully at the room we were in and then close our eyes. He asked us questions about what we could still see. Bardon wrote that, if you practised, you would see a room in all its details with your eyes shut, but he suggested a much easier task: to look at a flower, close your eyes, bring it to the forefront of your mind, see it in all its detail. If you could do that, very possibly the flower would materialize. I tried. I found that I could sit quietly with a still mind, almost as empty as a cloudless sky, but visualizing was very difficult.

Concurrent with my ascetic practices was a feeling of voluptuous sensuality that I satisfied now and then. Sinclair insisted that I take him into town every afternoon to check whether his money had arrived. One afternoon, he exited American Express with a young man in tow, shouldering a large backpack and a guitar. Roger was a muscular South African on a European holiday, with jet-black hair and the most intense violet-blue eyes veiled by long dark lashes. He seemed a bit shy. Sinclair spoke Afrikaans with him and then suggested he come and see my house, since it was a work of art by two great artists. Up at the house, we drank retsina, talked, ate, and Sinclair asked Roger to play his guitar. I couldn't resist Roger. He stayed on for a few days after Sinclair left. We fell in love with each other. I didn't want him to leave, and he asked me to come to South Africa with him.

Then he was gone, leaving only the memory of his blue, blue eyes. Sinclair wrote a poem about our meeting.*

We had no telephone. People just appeared at my blue gate, announced by Cleo's tumultuous welcome. Iannis, the dancing electrician, with whom I had had so much pleasure in Mykonos, arrived with a friend on a short leave from his military service. Would I like to join them for an evening of Rebetiko? He'd taught me the steps to this wonderfully sexy dance, and I remembered well enough to dance in front of a crowd of plate-smashing Greeks. Afterwards, I told him that I couldn't take him home at this late hour. Two years before, Takis and I had found a strange hotel not very far away. Iannis and I enjoyed a wonderfully erotic night in this hotel built for sex, with dim red lights, bidets and discretion. In the morning, we were the only couple still there.

On 22 December 1965, I was twenty-six years old and had spent almost seven years with Takis,

* Published in *A Cathedral of Angels & Luna Park: A Dual Anthology* by George Dillon Slater and Sinclair Beiles, Athens: Anglo-Hellenic Publishing, 1974.

who was due to arrive on 26 December. I hoped the magic number seven would make it a magic year. Ruby gave the house warmth and a happy aura. Cleo had puppies that Thanos kept carrying off, which Cleo would gently return to her bedding.

Now I can't wait till Takis comes. I don't feel unhappy he is not here, nor impatient, nor worried about my work, but, somehow, very satisfied with everything and full of the pleasures of life. My senses feel so happy with my surroundings that I feel high.

It was completely predictable. I should have known that Takis would not like Ruby, that he would not appreciate having an intelligent, educated, older woman running our household. Perhaps he was jealous of my relationship with her and the freedom her looking after things gave me. He told me that she put on airs, that she thought she was better than his family. He placed a paraffin heater in her room that nearly suffocated her. In short, he quarrelled with her after the first week and I lost my thoughtful companion.

Takis left for Paris early in January and my days

became full of energy and optimism again. There were still problems to solve to make the house more comfortable, but we now had electricity, and I had established a routine of care for Thanos, giving me much more time for my own work. I wrote poems and made poem cylinders and cones.

Jan 14th — I am feeling very happy and so grateful for everything which surrounds me. Most of the time, I don't realise that this house and the land around it are mine. When I think of this, I feel overwhelmed — how do other people own so much? Perhaps they never think about it. I think that if it was all taken away, I would not despair. I don't really feel attached, and I want to remember that. I feel happy about my work and am beginning to really like the cylinders that I thought I had lost interest in. I told Hyde, an American writer living in Athens, that it takes me a year to change one line in my work. Now I understand that to make changes, even the slightest, one needs to study and think it over from all angles.

I look into the mirror and see my face. Is it really mine? I don't feel that familiar with it.

My face disappears in the mirror.

My face becomes empty mask.

My life my mind leaves my face.

My eyes become blank.

My mind goes into my head.

To the top.

The feeling is very strange.

I love the feeling of my mind leaving my body.

I am not afraid.

Perhaps the painful period of work on myself was now bearing fruit.

Working in Paris

In March, my mother and André looked after Thanos in Ponte Tresa. Takis was in New York, and I could work freely in the rue Saint-André des Arts studio. Takis had asked Raymondos to help me, which I appreciated, even if we often quarrelled.

One day, one of my small motors stopped turning, forcing Raymondos to take it apart. I remarked that he was too rough. Offended, Raymondos abandoned me, leaving bits of motor on the workbench. I'd never even seen the inside of a motor but, smarting with guilt and annoyed that he'd left, I slipped the tiny bronze gears on to the correct pins and put the motor back together. I understood that there were no mysteries inherent in motors, which gave me a new sense of freedom and independence.

The size of Paris in comparison with Athens made me feel anonymous. I felt sexually frustrated, resulting in encounters I later regretted, fast fucks with strangers I never would see again, without the warmth and affection I'd experienced in Greece. I tried to divert my bubbling sexual energy into spiritual energy, but my body had ideas and needs of its own.

During this stay in Paris with Takis's small studio all to myself, I completed several works heading in different directions, finally understanding that lines and words were interchangeable. I worked on my own for a month but, when I stopped, I felt empty and unsure about what I had made, although I had no doubts about what I'd learned while working.

April 11th – Making a cone, I added many coloured lines. I was fascinated by the beauty of the colours themselves. Then I realised that it was too much, all those beautiful details did not make a vibrating whole. I understood, not without pain, that I would have to cut the colours with black to get a whole. It struck me that I could apply this to life. I began, for the first time, to understand colours deeply, I felt them as signals or words, each colour sending out a message, so instead of words, I could easily put colours on my cones. Letters by themselves suggest words, g or ii or s or ooop. I feel meaning in them, sometimes more than in the word itself, because words, today, are used without power. Everything has to be split like they split the atom in order to live again. I want to split myself and other people, split words and matter.

Before leaving Paris, Takis had given me a present of a few cork cones that he had ordered for me from a company that made the cork balls for his work with magnets. I had made smaller wooden *Poemcones* in Greece, but I preferred the larger cork cones. Feeling that Lennie's concise rhythmic poems were made for my cones, I started with *Sky Never Stops*, positioning the words of the poem in repetitive rings spaced to accentuate the rhythm of the whole poem.

Sky Never Stops
Inner Space

Outer Space
Same Distance*

I also painted three cork cones with layered rings of colour.

My father, who was now importing Japanese cameras, gave me a three-inch telescope to look at the moon and the planets. In Greece, I'd painted a line of colour on a spinning mesh cylinder, thinking of Saturn. The many-coloured rings on the cones were connected to what I'd been reading about stellar spectra. I was fascinated by how the dark lines in each star's spectrum told the intimate story of the matter it was made of. Each striped cone was a story of light.

I'd just finished these colourful works when David Medalla sent the Brazilian artist Sergio Camargo to see my work. This charming man looked more successful bon vivant than artist. His own works were geometric reliefs, always painted a pure white. He was full of praise for my *Poemcones*, but said the striped cones looked quite ethnic. Instead of asking what he meant, I thought his comment was a

* Poem by Leonard D. Marshall.

criticism. My intention was far from making ethnic or folkloric works and I disliked having my work misunderstood. I couldn't get over Camargo's view and I overpainted the striped cones white, to reuse them. It was the 1990s before I would return to the 'ringed spectrum cones', my *Striped Koans*.

I explored two new directions for my *Echo-Lights*. Instead of using thick blocks of Perspex, lit by a projector with a turning lens, I fabricated a frame with a white back and a clear Perspex front, on which I injected lenses in appropriate patterns. Change and movement came from small lights set in the frame and controlled by a cam-switch sequencer that changed the direction of the light. My first, quite hand-made, one was in a group exhibition, *Art Electric* (1966), at the Ileana Sonnabend Gallery in Paris. I came a bit late to the opening, to find that my work had not been plugged in. Terribly upset by this humiliation, I asked why, only to be told that they didn't know its voltage and had not dared to plug it in in case it ran on 115 volts — which made me realize how unprofessional I'd been.

In the second development of *Echo-Lights*, I made a series of clear Perspex discs, again injecting each one with polymer lenses. Three were stacked on top of each other and sat on a turntable. The idea was that, as they turned, the reflections from the lens patterns would move and change in relation to each other. They were made and shown at Signals Gallery in London during spring 1966 after Paul Keeler and David Medalla invited me to London to take part in a group exhibition and to discuss a solo exhibition for the following autumn. I finished off the work in the gallery, photographed in the process by Clay Perry, who beautifully documented the events and artists in Signals.

David introduced me as a great artist to the other artists and poets, including the poet John Sharkey and the artist Gustav Metzger, whose *Destruction in Art Symposium* I had, unfortunately, just missed. I also met Italian artist Pia Pizzo, whom I would get to know quite well once I'd moved to London. David spoke with great enthusiasm about my interest in science and my work with light. I felt thrilled to be part of this wonderfully ebullient group.

London was alive with music, art and fashion. People were more nonconformist. No one seemed to mind what you looked like. Prices for clothes were so much lower than in Paris, and they were exciting and wild. Miniskirts were in and I couldn't resist buying a few outfits. Paris was staid in comparison; women still wore skirts just below the knee. Back in Paris, an English girlfriend and I wore our minis to the Coupole. Heads turned and one or two men clapped. We pretended to ignore the attention, although secretly basking in it, as more and more people stood up and joined in the applause.

I returned to the camera shop on the Boulevard Beaumarchais, where I'd been regaled with a vision of spectral joy. In the window, the same trays of optical glass prisms were still displayed. Clear prisms or prisms with black-painted sides, cut in so many different shapes. I wanted to buy them all, but I could only afford a few to make my first prism works, identical prisms in simple geometric sequences of light, on velvet-covered trays: *Periscope Eye*, *Rays*, *White Mirror*, *White Magic* and *Spectrum*.

On 22 April, Takis returned unexpectedly: and now it will be quite hard for me to work. I feel confused about what I will do until I go to Greece. I want to make an experiment with mercury — like splitting the atom. Mercury split up by speed of rotating disc – finds equilibrium when disc slows down.

I quarrelled with my mother. She is terrible, turning Thanos against me. Putting doubt and sadness into his little heart. I am so angry with her. It is not a good day. It is not a good day. It is not a good day

I quarrelled with my mother because she couldn't keep the nannies I hired to look after Thanos. It was always up and down with my parents. I should have been grateful to them for looking after my little son, but his custody was the fulcrum for all our grievances. When my father became too aggressive about my way of life or my relationship with Takis, I threatened to let my mother have Thanos. When my mother had Thanos, I didn't want him spoiled with toys or sweets. My parents rarely complained, happy to look after their usually well-behaved grandson, who was quite adorable.

I agreed to meet my mother at the end of June in Cannes, from where Thanos and I would take a boat to Athens. I would be in Paris for two more months and I had work to do. Harald Szeemann had invited me to exhibit in *White on White*, a group exhibition at the Bern Kunsthalle, which looked at artists connected to or inspired by the Bauhaus.

I made a thin clear Perspex drum about two centimetres deep and tried my experiment with mercury, spinning it around at high speed, but the results were not what I'd hoped for. The glob of mercury did break up into the smallest droplets, but they seemed lifeless. I carefully stored the disappointing mineral and washed the drum out thoroughly. When I rinsed it with clear water, I let it sit on a piece of white paper on the workbench to dry. Almost immediately, I noticed small, trembling droplets of water forming on the inner surface of the disc, projecting reflections and shadows on the white background. Of course! Water was the answer. Simple pure water. In 1963, I had jotted down in my notebook *Notes on Molecular Radiation Paintings and Vibrations* that to avoid using the polymer to make plastic lenses, one solution might be:

> In a transparent cavity already fabricated inside
> the Plexiglass, inject water or oil or both, from
> behind with a hypodermic needle.

Another solution presented itself to me in the aftermath of the failed experiment. I'd thought of oil in 1963 and, either remembering or rediscovering that, I purchased some light liquid paraffin and dropped a small spoonful into the water. It behaved as a kind of glue, creating a preferential wetting surface on the underside of the top disc, so that the condensing droplets proliferated and remained there like permanent dewdrops until the disc or drum was picked up and shaken, when the whole process began anew. This new work was white on white, and I decided to take it to Bern.

Takis had been invited but didn't want to go and he asked me to install his work. Paul Keeler came for the opening, since several Signals artists were in the show, and we spent time together. We agreed that I would have a show in November. David and I would share the gallery, and Paul promised to find me a studio and cover my expenses for making new works. I was ecstatic with anticipation.

It was interesting to be in Bern for a large museum exhibition, although Harald Szeemann was not yet the famous curator he would become. The atmosphere he created at the Kunsthalle was lively and exciting. He was always accessible, behaving more like an artist than the director of a public gallery. He came over to check on my work. I'd installed it as well as possible, given that it didn't have a spotlight of its own, but I felt overwhelmed by the other, much larger, works.

I explained the work to Harald, who said, 'Your work is experimental and that's interesting, Liliane, but for group shows, never bring small works.'

Once again, I realized how naive and inexperienced I was. But after two years of solitude in Athens, my life was exploding with new experiences and a plethora of ideas for new works.

From Bern, I went to visit my father in Geneva. He spent his days in his office and his nights, when not gambling, in front of his television set constantly switching channels or reading with the radio at full volume, until he fell asleep without turning anything off. By 1966 he had met his last love, Gisela Bonner, a tall, lanky German woman with a matter-of-fact attitude. She was my age, did not live in Geneva and was therefore not always around. When she was, she prepared the things he liked to eat, all unhealthy. He was convinced that I despised him because he was a businessman, but nevertheless did not make the effort to spend time with me. There was always something else he had to do or someone he had to see. It had been that way ever since I was a teenager, when I lived in Lugano but spent my holidays with him.

The occasions when we were alone were rare, but they were memorable and precious. Like the afternoon in 1958 when he visited me in the pension in Geneva, where I was boarding because I couldn't live under the same roof with his second wife, Lourdes. I was studying on my own for A Levels to obtain the Cambridge certificate in four months, so that I could leave for Paris in the autumn. We spent a precious hour together in which he told me how much he admired me for my drive and self-discipline, for my talents that he assured me I had in abundance: 'I am counting on you to fulfil yourself, to accomplish what I never managed. You have it in you. I will always be there for you.' Those may not have been his exact words, but I was touched, not realizing the responsibility it gifted me. Eight years later, I felt that I was beginning to fulfil the promise, but he did not agree. His main complaint was that I had not got a degree. He'd said he would never accept Takis, but because of Thanos, he now liked his son-in-law.

I'd brought a small piece of hash and a little pipe, thinking it might make my stay more bearable. Before he returned home, I smoked a little and it was amazing how well we got on. His complaints, taunts and aggression made me laugh, which diffused the tension enough that we were able to talk about our lives. My being relaxed and accepting allowed him to relax.

At the weekend, he took me to the Poppers. Leo Popper was an old business colleague who had become very wealthy – while my father, a more brilliant man, never attained more than brief moments of financial success. I disliked the brash, ignorant and physically repulsive Poppers and their six spoiled children. We sat in their large garden in the hot sun around a white metal table, drinking white wine. I played with my glass, absorbed by the pure reflection the wine cast on the table. I remembered that I had some clear marbles. The next day, I sat on the sunny balcony, playing with the exquisite reflections cast by the marbles as they rolled across the table. This was my next work: clear Perspex balls moving at random on a rotating white surface. I had another disc in Greece and couldn't wait to try it out.

I met my mother and Thanos in Cannes and boarded a boat for Haifa, which would take us to Athens. On the way it stopped at Naples, where we disembarked and had a day to wander around the old city. I have a beautiful photograph of Thanos on an ornate balcony, tall for his age and looking and behaving older than his four years. People kept asking whether we were siblings, which made him very proud.

At Gero Vouno, I realized by the look of the house that I'd been absent too long. Worse still, Cleo was in a veterinary clinic. We had still not unpacked when my usual *piratis* drove up and introduced me to his brother-in-law: 'I told him about your house, and he wanted to see it.' As they walked in, Thanos came to see who had arrived. The brother-in-law exclaimed, 'What a beautiful boy!' In Greece, it was customary to immediately follow praise of somebody's child by saying he or she should live for you, a traditional protective wish for a long life. The man forgot to say it. I couldn't believe my eyes as I clearly saw Thanos wilt. Later that evening, he went down with a high fever. I had to call my mother-in-law to cure him of the evil eye. The next time I saw my *piratis*, I mentioned this. He apologized profusely and told me that his brother-in-law had a son of the same age who had polio.

I wanted to try out the clear balls moving on a simple white disc, but the only disc I had in Gero Vouno was a thin drum filled with water and a little paraffin oil, similar to the one I had exhibited in Bern. I placed the disc on a small turntable and carefully put the clear marbles on its surface, adding a larger clear Perspex ball. What I saw amazed me. The balls were moving magnifying lenses, enlarging the lunar landscape of the droplets, their shadows and reflections. A few days later, Gregory Corso visited and peered closely at the shifting shadows and reflections, mesmerized.

Takis returned in July. He told me that he'd met my friend Juliet and they'd fucked a few times. He'd told her how he missed me, while she urged him to leave me. He said he needed to warn me that she was not a real friend, and he wasn't interested in her for anything more than easy sex. At first, I thought he was making it up. He had more than likely fucked her, but that she had begged him to drop me and stay with her was hard to believe. Was he telling me this to hurt me, to let me know that even my best friends would deceive me? He told me she'd followed him to Athens.

The summer before, I had spoken to Juliet about Takis. She'd asked whether he was a good lover. Teasing her, I replied, 'Why don't you try him out?' She appeared shocked and insisted that she'd never do such a thing. No doubt I'd whetted her appetite. I wrote to her, telling her that Takis had told me about Paris, that I didn't want it to come between us. We'd been friends since we were twelve. What had just happened wasn't important. She returned a poisonous letter, letting me know that she'd never felt comfortable with me.

This event affected me more than I realized or wished to admit. I could no longer sleep with Takis. I felt repelled by his touch. I told myself that it was not because he'd fucked my best friend and destroyed my relationship with her. Takis believed that interruptions to our life together would not change anything. But during those long intervals alone I had found my feet, my own rhythm, and it was not compatible with his. After a few unhappy weeks, we agreed to go our separate ways and Takis left.

In September I would be driving to London,

and I was not at all sure when I would return. I felt as if everything I had created in Gero Vouno had now been thrown up in the air. I found it hard to believe what Takis had done. And Juliet! Had she felt envious of me all those years? Did she want to replace me, to be me?

I had been offered a show in London and would have to prepare new works. I tried to think constructively, but emotionally I was in turmoil. I needed to leave Gero Vouno, but I wasn't yet ready to leave Greece. I decided to spend my last month in Greece on my own, exploring the country and giving myself some breathing space.

I booked Thanos on to a plane to Geneva. It turned out that Harold Norse, whom I knew well from the Beat Hotel, was on the same flight. I knew that Thanos would be looked after by the stewardess, but I asked Harold to sit next to him, thinking he might distract my four-year-old. Harold was delighted and said he'd take good care of him. Thanos told me later that Harold was so terrified of flying he'd had to give him courage during the whole flight.

Since moving to Gero Vouno, Cleo had been my constant companion and fierce protector. I felt safe with her. She came with me to Athens on the bus. When I danced, she barked — I wasn't sure whether she wanted to join in. When we walked back up the hill in total darkness, she growled if she sensed another presence. I often thought that, in a past life, she must have been a human being. When I looked at a wall-hung life-size photograph of Takis's father, with thick curled moustache and hat, formally attired in black suit and white cravat, Cleo studied it then started to whine, as if she wanted to speak to him. In Mykonos, she slept under my bed and, trembling, didn't move until I did. I thought she wouldn't survive six months in British quarantine. A friend put me in touch with a man who owned Cleo's brother, an identical black shepherd. Sadly, I gave her away. Just before I left Athens, I spotted Cleo sitting in the back of a red convertible sports car, an identical black dog next to her, both enjoying the breeze. I called out her name, but she didn't even turn her head.

My plan was to spend the month driving around Crete. Takis sent money to Giorgos, who accompanied me to a used car lot. I saw the car of my dreams, a bright yellow Willys jeep, a convertible cabriolet. Giorgos insisted I buy a second-hand

VW Beetle, a choice I regretted. On the overnight boat trip, I slept on the deck. Stretched out next to me was a young American poet, another Roger, with whom I marvelled at the Milky Way.

August 8th – In the ruins of Knossos, I am disorientated. They have over restored . . . changing the ancient vibrations – I found this disturbing, but it was beautiful . . . On the way to Malia, a wonderful, deserted beach . . . Swimming naked with Roger, I wish he was my other Roger . . . I felt I needed to travel with someone, and he seemed quite nice, so I chose him. I would have preferred to come with someone I already knew, but all my advances failed . . . We are in Francocastello . . . 'God is raining,' says the old lady. 'He has no other work to do,' answers the boy.* Evangelis has a café with built-on plastered benches . . . he gives all he has: grapes, figs, bread, beans. We all drink wine at night and Evangelis recites 'mantinadas'. The Cretans speak melodically.

* 'O theos breixei.' 'Den exei kai tipota alo na kanei.'

They are poets born. I went to El Greco's birthplace. All his colours were there.

In Chania, we met novelist Charles Haldeman on the balcony of a café overlooking the sea. The two men discussed poetry and language. Charles said a writer must know his language intimately. I realized I had lost the use of my maternal tongue, but which language was mine? I could never be a writer, since my use of English was tentative; I did not have a wealth of words on the tip of my tongue. I wondered if Roger would become an established poet. He could have mentors in a way that a woman never could. Women had lovers; they had girl-friends in whom they could confide and share their dreams, but who would surely betray them, if only to have the good opinion of a man.

I quickly noticed that Roger was aggressive and disparaging towards me. He had a pretentious ego and he paid for nothing, which overrode the practicality of having a man to travel with. After ten days, I dumped him.

Every day is a week because I am moving . . .
As I move, 'light and radiation' from many new

and different images (places, objects, people) are fed into my brain and my conception of time changes . . . what is our conception of time and what time absolute? Do energy and matter exist separately in space and in time, or is spacetime one and the same, like a reversible raincoat?

I gave a lift to two French medical students who didn't speak a word of Greek. We drove through a fantastic landscape of multiplying velvet bleached-ochre hills, a river of soft silver-green olive trees in so many different shapes. With the darkening of night, I decided we had to stop at the next taverna. It was full of local people, who teased an askomandoura* player, disrespecting his art. But he played beautifully, and they danced. We bought him food and drink, and I ended up sleeping on the roof with eight male strangers.

On the way back to Heraklion, I drove through a dry river bed, full of small stones, after which I had trouble with my gear shift and heard a clunk. I stopped the car. The engine had fallen on to the road. We had to tie it up with rope and limp into

* Small bagpipes.

Heraklion in third gear, with no reverse. The garage said the crankshaft had snapped in two.

End of August, and I was back alone in Gero Vouno, having read Hoyle on the boat. Contemplating distance, parsecs and infinite space made me feel like nothing. I was feeling lonely but I wanted to overcome my need for a 'someone'. I tried to organize my things, to take only the necessary. I thought I would be returning. This was my only real home, so much of it built by me. I gave Takis's brother Vassilis some large paintings he said he liked. I gave many of the couture dresses my father had bought me to Titika's daughter, Maria.

> September 6th — Three days of hash, sex and unloosening . . . . I notice that, when my body emits vibrations of desire, there is no receiver. Men fear these vibrations, but as soon as they are cooled and my body at ease, many men appear and I read desire in their eyes . . . I let myself be completely absorbed by my own desire . . . until my ego did disappear . . . my lust transformed into something else. Burt came up to the house and we spoke all night and all morning.

Paul, Maria, and Burt came to the house, and we looked at my new work with water. They were very excited. I shook it – the lenses dissolved, leaving streaks, formless reflections. I saw them as interstellar clouds of gas forming into stars – they slowly form into spherical droplets – water and oil, matter, is formless, but electrostatic forces attract the water to the Plexiglass, slowly condensing into droplets, just as hydrogen clouds condense, subject to gravitational forces, into near round bodies. I saw how from such a simple thing as my disc, one can see the forces at play in the universe.

Destination London

AUTUMN 1966

I left Greece from Igoumenitsa, alone, as I had entered her the very first time six years earlier. I drove through verdant northern Greece, stopping to look at the grandure of Meteora. I didn't like the north as much as the south of Greece, preferring the sun-bleached, brush-covered hills to green, every Greek's favourite colour. I drove to Geneva through the gnarled olive groves of Puglia, stopping to visit Caresse in Rocca Sinibalda, and then on to Assisi to see the magnificent Giotto frescos in the Basilica, the innocent beginning of perspective, where I had the rare privilege of being alone. I also wanted to see the *Madonna del Parto*, Piero della Francesca's profound painting of the pregnant Madonna that was just outside Monterchi. I had to find the caretaker, who kindly came and opened the small chapel for me, and, as in Assisi, I could absorb in silence the harmonious composition and delicate colours of this deeply spiritual painting.

I had not only learned to speak Greek in Athens, I had also learned how to work with other people. Building Gero Vouno had taught me to work with a wide range of craftsmen, to think through what I wanted to have made, to sketch or draw it, to discuss with them how they thought best to make it and turn that over in my mind before agreeing. To discuss the cost of what I wanted, even to bargain, and, once agreed, to supervise and make sure the job was completed and delivered. I had learned a great deal and enjoyed working with people in Greece, who, although they had little material wealth compared to other Europeans, were people of great warmth, generosity and kindness.

I remained in Geneva for three weeks, looking after Thanos. I had agreed with my parents that Thanos would live with my father in Geneva until I could find a place of my own in London. I told Thanos that soon we would live together again and saw his little face light up with excitement.

Driving to Paris, where I would stay for a few days, I realized that my journey to London had taken me through the very places that had been important to me on my first trip to Greece in 1960. In an almost ritualistic way, I had stopped to see Caresse, driven through northern Italy to Geneva and across the Jura to Paris, where I met Julien Blaine, who enthusiastically showed me the photographs of my *Poemcones* and *Poem Machines* he had published in his magazine, *Approches*, and asked me to consign to him two works for an exhibition of concrete poetry he was curating in Madrid. With this encouraging news and a feeling that my life was about to change, I drove to Calais to board the ferry for London.

Who is Silvana Bismarck?

I have only begun my story, so this coda is an end to a beginning. In Italian *coda* means 'tail'. It is a strange tail that comes straight after the head, the kind of tail that would only figure in the Exquisite Corpse drawings of the surrealists. It may therefore be appropriate to share a surreal dream I had some-time in 1994.

I am standing in front of my house, looking up, when I see my mother leaning out of a second-floor window, silently waving to me. Only then, I notice cracks appearing in the wall below, spreading fast across it like the traces of a long-dead Virginia Creeper. With a fearsome sound of collapsing walls, the house begins to crumble, almost in slow motion, parts of it still hanging in the air. My mother tumbles out of the window as the house crashes down in a storm of stone and dust, leaving only a smoking heap. Numb with horror, I feel I have lost everyone and everything, including my name.

I awoke, still in the haze of the lingering dream, and I heard these words: 'I will give myself a new name, Silvana Bismarck.'

I liked the sound of this name and dreamily I decided that I should write an autobiography with the title: *Silvana Bismarck Speaks*.

Finally. Since women usually listen, while men do all the speaking. Or perhaps because I wanted to know more about myself, that self I had lived in and with, but who also existed through the sensations received from the world outside herself.

I had to begin with my parents, but I hardly knew anything of their early life, in their fabled past in Europe. They said that everything in Europe was better, the food, the culture, so lacking in America, so much more elegant until the menace of Hitler.

But who was Silvana Bismarck?

From birth, we accumulate names with the attachments that bind us to people, to places, to the material world. The one we are given at birth and the others, adopted or chosen. I had a few: Pupi, Liliane Segall, Nahil Lages, Liliane Line, Liliane

Lijn, Liliane Vassilakis and Liliane Lijn again. Having my name changed and then choosing my own was the result of movements and upheavals, whether geographic or internal. They were the markers on the path leading out of the labyrinth, the emotional maze of my genealogical past, my hidden memories of parental misadventures and my own stumbling beginnings.

Moving through this labyrinth of names, I had become an artist. I could now easily understand why I would, on awakening from a nightmare, give myself the name Silvana from the Latin *silva*; myths of sylvan nymphs, the damp and green forest, the many faces of nature, the feminine.

But why choose Bismarck, the surname of the brilliant Prussian politician who masterminded the unification of Germany in 1871 and served as its first chancellor until 1890, in which capacity he dominated European affairs for two decades? Does this designation simply signify male society, authority, power? I decided that Silvana Bismarck was a meeting of the feminine, of intuition and imagination, of nature on the one hand with the dominant power of male society on the other. Perhaps I was a struggling combination of these two worlds, my mother inside me and my father moving briskly in the light of day.

As a woman, I continually felt a dichotomy between my brain and my body. They were not in sync; I seemed to function either as one or the other. The solution seemed to be to compartmentalize and, as many other people, I did endeavour to keep my work separate from my emotional life. I still felt a definite split between a male brain and a female body. Why, I wondered, couldn't my brain be female?

From birth, society confirmed that break, with its rigid differentiation between genders, and in 1950s America, where I grew up, male was the default sex.* Everything was said and written in 'his' name. 'He' was the default pronoun to such an extent that, as a girl, I took it for granted that, in some strange way, I was he. I did not feel any confusion about my sexuality, my body that, even before menstruation, and certainly once that had struck at the age of twelve, utterly convinced me I was female with all the libido and sexual longings

* From *Invisible Women* by Caroline Criado Perez, Chatto & Windus, 2019.

for what appeared to be the opposite sex. But my mind ranged more freely than was expected from a girl and later from a woman. At every stage of my development, I felt the constrictions, the prohibitions, the restraints applied to my gender. The easiest path on offer was through the body, using appearance, beauty, sexuality, but there was hardly anything easy about that. Consider the most famous woman in America in the 1950s: Marilyn Monroe, who committed suicide aged thirty-six.

As a child, I sang to the wind with my head stretched outside the back window of our car; later, at camp or school, I was always chosen to sing the main part in the operettas we performed. I thought of becoming a jazz singer, but my father urged me to go to drama school instead. Both these professions would have had me out front, using my body as my tool. I preferred to use my mind, to remain invisible behind the product of my making. I began by painting, but even that felt too corporeal, too sensual, overwhelming my senses with its enticing odours and colours. Drawing was more of a mental exercise, a meditation, while also a skill. And drawing led me to research and invention. I had found some kind of balance through the sensuality of the materials I chose to work with, even if I often required the help of engineers and craftsmen to visualize my ideas.

I've exhibited my works widely and made numerous large-scale public works, and the spring of 2024 saw the opening of my first solo museum exhibition. It was held in Munich at the Haus der Kunst, travelling to mumok in Vienna and then to Tate St Ives. This solo museum show has been a long time coming, not only because of my gender, but also because of the large spectrum of my artistic practice and my interest in science and technology, which was out of step with the main directions in the art world at earlier stages of my career.

In the autumn of 1966, I arrived in London in my VW Beetle, having driven from Athens, for an exhibition at the Signals Gallery, an adventurous space run by artist David Medalla and his practical friend Paul Keeler, only to find it closed, the two of them having taken refuge in Scotland. Although brimming with exciting events, London seemed cold and dismal, but I put myself to work and developed the prototype I had made just before leaving Greece, a work showing the forces at play in the universe. I called it *Liquid Reflections*, since it consisted of a hollow rotating Perspex disc containing a liquid, on the surface of which two Perspex balls moved following the centrifugal pull of the spinning disc and the gravitational force exerted by the curvature of the disc's surface. I was mesmerized by the reflections and shadows cast by the changing shapes of water inside the disc. The balls appeared to dance across its surface, magnifying the changing lunarscape of reflections and shadows of condensing water droplets.

When first in London, I imagined that I would, at some point, return to New York. However, my totally unexpected meeting with a sexy Englishman in the still-swinging year of 1969 would change my mind. This unpretentious, tall young man with his wild shock of red hair had no connection with the world I moved in, having just returned from California with a BA in Economics. He was warm, energetic and intelligent, and when he first held my hand, I knew he was the man for me.

Stephen and I were married in 2016, after a suitably long engagement of forty-seven years, during which we brought up my first son, Thanos, and managed to have two more children, who both now have children of their own.

Looking back at my twenties, I realize the odd coincidences of life that formed the pattern that I call myself. Meetings and choices, often completely random or made in the moment, that I slid into so easily. In one of my notebooks, I wrote: 'my life was a house that I was building brick by brick'. Every brick I laid determined whom I became. But did I lay all the bricks? Didn't some just fall into place? I'd made conscious decisions. I decided I wanted to become an artist, much against the better judgement of my father, who wished so profoundly that I continue my studies at university, either in literature or philosophy. Archaeology was our compromise, and the short time that I spent looking at the images of Egyptian and Greek temples, at the Khmer figures in the Musée Guimet in Paris, cast threads deep into my subconscious, many-coloured threads that wove their way into my life's work. I remember my desperation at not being able to dissolve my ego, and my belief in the possibility of achieving enlightenment.

My friend the art writer Alastair Mackintosh, with whom I realized the first *Power Game* at the Royal College of Art as a performance for the International Festival for Chilean Liberation (1974), believed that pleasure was the enlightened path, whereas the physicist Viktor Vajtal believed that pain was the true path. Viktor took me to his Zen meditation classes, conducted by a fierce-looking man with long hair and beard. I found sitting cross-legged very painful and could hardly walk on my numb legs after the thirty-minute 'sesshin', when we all walked silently in a circle for five or ten minutes before sitting for another meditation. Alastair's reaction when I told him about it was, 'Your work is your meditation.'

Although my artistic practice throughout the 1960s and 70s was inspired by my interest in science and Buddhism, my ideas came from what I saw around me. In the late 70s, I healed the split I felt between male and female through an intense period of drawing with the aim of creating a new image of the feminine. This led to my incorporating soft materials in my sculptures, increasingly large female figures, and finally my archetypes or goddesses.* At the time I wrote in my notebook:

The return to the body is not a passing fashion.

The return is a long voyage made across

* *Lady of the Wild Things* (1983) and *Woman of War* (1986).

landscapes of the mind where the body had long ago dissolved to the blue ether of sky dreams or taken on strange forms, a myriad of forms spewed as in The Magic Queene from the bowels of the Earth. The bowels of the Earth was and still is the womb of Ereshkigal, her Queendom, the domain of death and the dead. From this place of disintegration all is born, is vomited up as lava pours from a volcano's crater – the great tits of the Earth.

I have become fascinated with memory, which is surely the best reason to write a memoir. When, in 1994, I discovered that I hardly knew anything about my parents' lives, my father, who had an extraordinary memory, had already died, so I plied my mother with questions. She told me stories, often repetitive, stories that she had heard from her mother, stories she half remembered from her own life, repeated and embroidered. I recorded her as she spoke, and while transcribing I realized how much I loved her voice, and I edited and made an artist's book, *Her Mother's Voice* (1996–98). I continued by making a film, interviewing all the people still alive who had known my parents (*Look a Doll!* 1998–2000).

In 1987, Stephen and I bought a ruined farmhouse near Umbertide in Umbria. When our local friend Alessandro Vestrelli organized an exhibition of my work in the town's museum, a fourteenth-century fortress,* I decided to record some memories of thirty diverse local people. I asked each person to describe the most intense memory from their childhood and was overwhelmed by the wealth of experiences, the intensity and colour of their lives. I felt honoured to be able to record their worlds.†

When my mother in her nineties developed Alzheimer's, she would point to *Her Mother's Voice* and, looking at me, say, 'You know my life.'

* Rocca di Umbertide.
† The three-screen film is *Voci d'Umbria* (2002).

Acknowledgements

I am grateful to Hilary Spurling for her invaluable advice and encouragement.

I thank my friend Bronac Ferran for suggesting that I offer my typescript to the Sarah Such Literary Agency. I had previously met Sarah under different circumstances, having given readings with her husband, the brilliant author Tony White.

I can't thank Sarah Such enough for her encouraging but firm early reading, insisting that my book be reduced in length and directing me to the best editors to do that. Thank you, Sarah, for taking me under your wing and giving my manuscript all your experienced and intelligent guidance to find the right publisher. Thank you, thank you, my dear Sarah. It is your expertise and amazing energy that has given us this result.

Warmest thanks to Alison Shakespeare, whose subtle pruning of my book reduced it to half its original length without changing the rhythm and voice of my writing.

I would also like to thank friends and colleagues who wrote delightful notes of praise regarding my work as an artist: Nicholas Serota, Hans Ulrich Obrist, Jennifer Higgie.

And thanks to my son Mischa Weiss-Lijn for his enthusiastic reading of my initial typescript, his suggestions for edits and, most of all, the list he made of all the extended periods I lived in New York, from my birth in 1939 to leaving the United States in 1954, and my frequent trips interrupting my living in New York in the 1960s. This list was essential to corroborate the dates I provided in my book.

'Liliane Lijn has been a unique and self-renewing force of creativity for six decades, amounting to an exceptional and unclassifiable career as a visual artist in many media, as well as a poet and a thinker' Marina Warner

'[*Liquid Reflections*] is not simply a record of the evolution of an artist, but a testament to the strength of spirit and imagination that allowed Lijn to develop her artwork in the face of structural sexism' Jennifer Higgie

'A revelatory account of a singular coming of age: a glittering portrait of the artist as a young woman' *Interalia Magazine*

ABOUT THE AUTHOR

Liliane Lijn is an artist and writer. From text-based kinetic sculptures to large, animated installations inspired by science, mythology and eastern philosophies, Lijn combines industrial materials with artistic processes to reimagine the female body. Her work is held in important public collections, including the Tate, the Victoria & Albert Museum, the British Museum and FNAC in Paris. She has been exhibited internationally since the 1960s, most recently in Electric Dreams at Tate Modern and in the major retrospective Liliane Lijn: Arise Alive at the Haus der Kunst, Munich, touring to mumok, Vienna and Tate St. Ives. Born in New York, Lijn subsequently lived in Lugano, Paris, New York and Athens before finally settling in London in 1967.